Digital Deceptions

Copyright © 2024 Tito Lugo MD
All rights reserved:
"Digital Deceptions"

The characters and events portrayed in this book are fictitious. Any similarity to real persons, living or dead, is coincidental and not intended by the author.

No part of this book may be reproduced, or stored in a retrieval system, or transmitted in any form or by any means, electronic, mechanical, photocopying, recording, or otherwise, without express written permission of the publisher.

Writer Guild of America East
Registration Number: 1369962
Registration Date: 04/21/2024

ISBN: 9798324726577

Cover: Oil painting "Lovers" by Lugo-Vicent - 2005

Printed in the United States of America

...an engrossing tale of digital intrigue and the perils of vanity...

Digital Deceptions
Tito Lugo MD©

I

The index finger, almost autonomous in its macabre dance, scrolled through images that, like fragments of a frivolous and exhibitionist society, slipped through social platforms. They were portraits of physical beauty, in black and white, silhouettes proclaiming an alien and distant aesthetic. Images of miraculous diets, like modern potions promising eternal youth. Photographs of a family vacation in the Belgian Congo, a superficial exoticism marred by the presence of domesticated gorillas, symbols of decadent opulence.

And so, they continued to parade literary achievements, verses laden with artificial pathos, other adventures designed for a platform hungry for instant and fleeting approval. All of it, a desperate cry for recognition, a confirmation of our existence, of our knowledge, of our ability to recognize and be recognized, good, creative, brimming with satire and black humor. It was the sustenance for a soul troubled by the lack of interest in its own being.

As my calloused finger continued its inexorable descent, I paused at the optical illusion of a young woman, offering her renewed body to the socionauts. She had remodeled her bust, her hips, and the result was a masterpiece of modern surgery. Her profile was flooded with 'likes', mostly from male fingers, reacting to her constant bodily insinuations online.

Eventually, I stopped following her, only to later learn that she had been asked out and then found slaughtered in a seedy motel. The place, a den of secrets, forbade video cameras and allowed entry to vehicles with tinted windows. No one cared who came and went as long as they paid. Thus, the beautifully reconstructed body of Amarilis lay, another victim of a debauchery that transcended mere physical violence.

She lay stretched out, lifeless and unaltered, on the rotating bed of the motel. Before any examination of injuries, it was confirmed that she had been violated, both vaginally and anally, according to forensic analyses of the fluids. There was male semen everywhere, including in the gastric juices. In other words, the murderer, like a predator masked in the shadows of everyday life, had woven a web of seduction around Amarilis. Through the same platforms that she had used to showcase her renewed body and her thirst for recognition, he had found a way to approach her. He had used her, exploiting her vulnerability and her desire to be seen, recognized, desired. In this act, he not only destroyed a body but also annihilated a dream, a hope, a quest for something more in life.

In this twisted scenario, journalists, voracious for a sensational story, wasted no time in capitalizing on the tragedy. The corpse of Amarilis, lying in a pool of her own blood, became the focus of unprecedented journalistic morbidity. The images of the scene, captured clandestinely, flooded the same social networks that, in life, had been the stage for her quest for recognition.

The irony was cruel. The same platforms that Amarilis had used to share moments of her life now served to exhibit her tragic end. The motel, the scene of the crime, turned into a kind of macabre theater. The owners, after notifying the tenants that their time had expired, were met with silence in response. The black Ford Bronco, which had entered with its occupant and victim, had disappeared into the darkness of the night.

Upon forcing the room's door, they encountered a Dantean scene they could never forget. The hastily taken photos began to circulate, feeding the public's voracious appetite for scandal. One journalist in particular, known for his work in the tabloid press, saw in these images a golden opportunity. Believing he had material for a Pulitzer, he began to spin his story, morbidly exploiting every detail.

The death of Amarilis, therefore, becomes a powerful symbol of contemporary relationships, where the virtual and the real often intertwine, with dangerous consequences. Her murder is not just an act of physical violence; it is also a reflection of a society that values individuals as objects, as images on a screen, stripping them of their humanity.

Officer Ernesto Prieto from Precinct Five took on the task of unraveling the mystery surrounding the cruel murder of Amarilis. With the meticulousness of an experienced hunter, he began his investigation at the most logical starting point in these modern times: Amarilis's social media. There, in the digital labyrinth, he hoped to find clues about her life before heading to the center of the island to interview her family.

Amarilis, whose beauty did not go unnoticed, lived with her biological parents. Her work life unfolded at a nursing home, where her presence was a light in the residents' routine. However, it was not all innocent admiration;

some of the elderly, in moments of clarity or confusion, dared to pinch her reconstructed posterior, to which Amarilis would respond with a scolding, a slap on the hands. She did not want relatives to see bruises on their family members housed in the health care home.

The news of her death shook the foundation of the facility. It was not only an emotional blow, the loss of someone beloved and respected, but also a logistical challenge, the search for a substitute for Amarilis, whose absence left a difficult void to fill. The meticulous nature of the crime, which seemed to be executed with surgical precision, added an additional level of horror and mystery to the case.

Officer Prieto, overwhelmed with emotions and thoughts, knew that the path to the truth would be fraught with obstacles. Each testimony, each memory of Amarilis, each digital interaction she had had, would be a piece of the puzzle he needed to assemble. In his quest for justice, Ernesto delved into a world where beauty, madness, and tragedy were inseparably intertwined, revealing the many facets of life and death in a world increasingly connected and, at the same time, disconnected from human reality.

Amarilis's humble family, plunged into an abyss of pain, faced the harsh reality of their only daughter's death. From childhood, Amarilis had dreamed of becoming a nurse, a desire inspired by the love and memory of her grandfather, who had played a crucial role in her upbringing. In a home where her parents worked tirelessly to provide her with a better future, Amarilis found in her grandfather not just care and love but also the inspiration for her future vocation.

Her aspiration was not just a career; it was a tribute to the one who had taught her the value of compassion and caring for others, especially those in their twilight years. The news of her tragic end hit the family like a devastating storm. Every corner of their home was filled with deep mourning, a mix of pain, disbelief, and anger at the cruel way Amarilis had met her end.

The tragedy of Amarilis transcended the mere fact of her murder; it was also the loss of a dream, of a future that promised love and care for those who, like her grandfather once did, depended on the kindness and skill of others. For her family, every memory of Amarilis was a reminder of what had been lost: a life dedicated to serving others, brutally and incomprehensibly cut short.

The lifeless body of Amarilis, now ethereally beautiful and tragic, lay in the cold, sterile autopsy room of the forensic institute. The bureaucratic reality and the backlog of work at the institute meant that it would be days before pathologists could perform the autopsy to determine the exact circumstances of her murder, based on the findings at the crime scene.

The image of Amarilis, naked and abandoned on the round motel bed, continued to haunt those who had seen the scene. The circular mirrors on the ceiling, silent witnesses to what should have been moments of pleasure and abandonment, now reflected an act of brutality and dehumanization. The room's layout, designed to amplify the joy of intimate encounters, had transformed into a stage of horror, a grotesque contrast between the intention of its design and the reality of its final use.

As Amarilis's body waited in the morgue, the investigation was in a forced pause. This interval, however, did not mean a halt in the search for answers. Officer Prieto and his team continued gathering information, interviewing potential witnesses, and reviewing nearby security camera footage. Every hour that passed without a complete autopsy was an hour lost in the race against time to catch the perpetrator.

As Officer Prieto delved into Amarilis's digital world, a new landscape of clues and possibilities opened up before him. The comments on social media, reflections of admiration, desire, and in some cases, disturbing obsession, provided a broad field for investigation. Among the public messages, Prieto found several individuals whose words crossed the boundaries of politeness and admiration into darker and more disturbing territory.

The comments ranged from harmless praise to more intense and direct insinuations. Some of these users seemed to view Amarilis not as a person, but as an object of desire, something to be possessed and consumed. Amarilis dodged these propositions with boldness and elegance, as evidenced by her public replies. But what happened in private messages, where conversations could take a more personal and possibly more sinister turn?

Officer Prieto knew that accessing this crucial information would require a court order—a special permit—to delve into the private messages for reasons linked to the crime investigation. This step was necessary not only because of the sensitive nature of the messages but also due to privacy and data protection laws. Aware of the importance of this data, Prieto moved to obtain the necessary authorization from the telecommunications board, knowing that every unread message could be the key to unmasking the murderer.

Officer Prieto faced one of the great complexities of the digital age: the ease with which identities could be masked on social media. Behind each pseudonym or anonymous profile hid a potential suspect, each one shielded by layers of falsehood and deception. Made-up email addresses, fictitious names, stolen or fabricated identities; the internet was a breeding ground for all kinds of individuals, from the most harmless to the most dangerous.

Upon receiving the report with details of the users who had sent private messages to Amarilis, Prieto realized the magnitude of the challenge ahead. The task was like looking for a needle in a haystack, a haystack made up of mountains of digital debris where every piece of information could be contaminated or irrelevant.

However, amidst this apparent hopelessness, Officer Prieto knew he had to keep a cool head and a clear focus. He began to categorize and analyze each message, looking for patterns, inconsistencies, or any detail that might point to a suspect. He knew that in investigations of this nature, sometimes the smallest detail could open the door to the truth.

Although the task was daunting, Officer Prieto was determined to leave no stone unturned. Every message, every online interaction was a potential clue that could bring him one step closer to solving the mysterious murder of Amarilis. In this maze of hidden identities and digital communications, the perseverance and sharpness of the officer would be his most valuable tools for uncovering the culprit and bringing justice to Amarilis's memory.

In his meticulous search for answers, Officer Prieto plunged into an exhaustive investigation, interviewing witnesses at the motel where Amarilis's body was found, speaking with relatives, and tracking connections on the young woman's social networks. However, despite his efforts, he was at a standstill, as baffled as on the first day. The only solid clue he had was the presence of a black Ford Bronco with tinted windows; a clue that, in its isolation, barely contributed to advancing the case.

In an era marked by rapid information dissemination and digital justice, the results of the police investigation were disappointing for Amarilis's family. The pain of their loss was compounded by the frustration of not getting answers, of not seeing justice for the young woman whose life had been cut so abruptly short.

Driven by their desperation and desire for justice, Amarilis's family demanded that federal authorities get involved. However, without evidence of kidnapping or a crime that crossed state jurisdictions, the federal authorities stayed on the sidelines, leaving the case in the hands of local police.

As time passed with no significant progress in the investigation, the pressure from Amarilis's family on the authorities only increased. They clung to the hope that, at some point, a crucial clue, an unexpected witness, or a revelation would emerge that could shed light on Amarilis's tragic fate.

Officer Prieto, although lost in a labyrinth of dead-end leads, remained committed to the case, aware that the key to solving the mystery could still be revealed. In this battle against time and the shadows of crime, each day without answers was a reminder of the urgency of his mission and the enduring pain of a family longing for justice for their lost loved one.

II

Alfredo Montesino, in a gesture of relaxed contemplation, lay extended on a beach chair at the Intercontinental Thalasso Hotel in Bora-Bora. His eyes, lost in the majestic central mountain, found in its silhouette a kind of ancestral peace. The kind waitress Ay, whose name resonated with the vital element of water in the native Polynesian language, had offered him a Mai Tai, that mix of tropical flavors which he accepted with a gesture of gratitude, feeling how the drink refreshed his soul as much as his body.

Surrounded by the 88 bungalows that spread their charm over the property, once owned by the famous actor Marlon Brando, Alfredo could not stop admiring the work of engineering and respect for nature that unfolded before him. Brando, in his vision, had achieved a perfect symbiosis between human comfort and environmental respect. Through PVC pipes 16 inches in diameter and 1.8 miles long to the bottom of the sea, he extracted the coldest, deepest water from the ocean acting as a natural siphon which, as it passed through the air conditioning ducts, provided ideal coolness to each of the bungalows, without the usual energy cost. Then, this water, slightly warmer but not contaminated, was returned to its oceanic origin.

This system, unique in the world, where the air conditioning of the bungalows used cold sea water from the depths of the sea, had captured Alfredo's imagination. Could this engineering marvel be replicated on his native island? He dreamed of implementing this harmonious coexistence between technology and the environment, a model where nature was not only used to benefit human beings but was also respected and preserved.

Alfredo Montesino, an expert in solving complex crimes, had gained fame and fortune throughout his career. One of his most notable cases was that of the serial killer on the expressway. Hilberto Santos, a being whose surname contradicted the nature of his acts, had become the nightmare of the island. For three years, he carried out thirteen meticulous and brutal murders, each targeted at members of the evangelical community, whom he considered his target for reasons deeply rooted in his twisted psyche. His crimes were characterized not only by the act of killing but by the barbarity with which he dismembered his victims in a hidden basement, to later scatter their remains on the island's busiest highway under the cover of darkness.

The first revelation of his atrocity came in the most macabre way possible: A driver, stopping on the highway to investigate what he believed to be a run-over animal, discovered in horror that he had stepped on a human hand. This discovery triggered a series of equally horrifying finds, as human pieces, brutally mutilated and disfigured by vehicles traveling at high speed, began appearing on the road. The remains, belonging to twelve more victims, were identified as members of the same religious community as the woman, which led to them being named the "twelve apostles" in a grotesque twist of the tragedy.

This case, one of the darkest and most complex that Montesino had faced, pushed him to the limits of his capacity as a detective. Not only did he have to track and understand the mind of a methodical and ruthless killer, but he also had to deal with the emotional and psychological impact of such horrific crimes. Solving this mystery required not only forensic skill but also a deep understanding of human psychology and a strong stomach to face the dismembered and re-mangled remains of innocent victims.

The hunt for Hilberto Santos became a race against time for Montesino, knowing that each day that passed could result in another lost life. This case not only tested his ingenuity as a detective, but also plunged him into a depth of human evil that would forever change his view of the world.

Alfredo Montesino's cunning led him to discover the connection between the gruesome crimes and a specific religious congregation. The common thread was the humiliating excommunication of Hilberto Santos by this church, an event that uncovered the motive behind his wave of terror. Rejected and tarnished, Hilberto turned into a being consumed by deep resentment, channeling it into a ruthless revenge against the members of the faith that had spurned him.

Capturing Hilberto was not a difficult task for a detective of Montesino's caliber. His arrest put an end to the nightmare that had been looming over the community, saving countless lives that otherwise might have fallen into the hands of this unhinged perpetrator.

The church's relief and gratitude towards Alfredo materialized in a generous stipend, rewarding the successful resolution of a case that had challenged and terrified society. This recognition was not only a testament to his skill and determination as a detective but also another chapter in his legacy of confronting and dismantling the deepest darkness of human criminality.

With this latest triumph, Alfredo Montesino not only reaffirmed his reputation as a master in solving complex cases but also demonstrated his ability to navigate the turbulent waters of the human psyche, unraveling hidden motivations and bringing justice to those whose voices had been silenced by terror.

Similarly, he solved the crime involving the Canadian businessman Adam Ashland, murdered under the instigation of his wife, Aurea Velez. Adam, having discovered Aurea's infidelity and disturbed by a private detective's report, had decided to divorce. According to the laws, Aurea would receive little in a divorce, but would inherit a fortune if Adam died. Informed of this, Aurea opted for murder.

Three years after the crime, a series of revealing letters reached Tony "The Butcher," which were payment claims from Alex Pombo, the hired assassin, to Aurea. Angel Marcel, whose brother had been wrongfully imprisoned for the murder, discovered these letters, and alerted the police, leading to his brother's release and Pombo's arrest. Aurea, meanwhile, had fled to Europe, married again, and had two daughters, but her suspicious behavior led her new husband to separate and take their daughters. Although authorities were monitoring her, they could not extradite her from Italy.

Finally, Alfredo Montesino, in a carefully planned operation, lured Aurea to Spain with a fake job offer. She was arrested at Barajas Airport in Madrid, thus closing one of the most dramatic and complicated chapters in Montesino's career.

Alfredo Montesino, hired by the family of the deceased businessman to investigate and capture the fugitive Aurea Velez, received a considerable reward for his successful work. This substantial sum was the reason he decided to take a well-deserved break from his detective duties, choosing the serenity and beauty of the Polynesian island of Bora-Bora as his temporary refuge. In this paradise, he sought not only rest and disconnection but also a moment of introspection and recharge before diving back into the world of criminal investigation.

Alfredo Montesino, now distanced from the shadows of his previous cases, found himself immersed in the serenity of Bora-Bora, but his mind could not completely detach from the mysteries he had unraveled in the past. As he watched the sunset reflected in the crystal-clear waters, a part of him remained tied to the labyrinths of crime and conspiracy he had left behind.

The peace of Bora-Bora, with its tranquil splendor, was suddenly disturbed for Alfredo Montesino. An unexpected sound, the tinkling of a text message, cut through the silence, pulling him back to the world he had tried to leave behind. The screen of his cell phone lit up his face with a cold light, announcing the arrival of a message from an old acquaintance in the dark world of criminal investigations. This contact, who had operated in the depths of crime and mystery just like Alfredo, carried a palpable urgency in his message.

The note was brief but loaded with gravity. It spoke of a new development in a case that had challenged the skills of the best detectives: the mysterious murder of Amarilis. This mention stirred an echo in Alfredo's memory, recalling a case that had captivated headlines and caused bafflement in police circles.

The text message read: "I need your help with a crime," signed by Agent Prieto, an old friend from the police academy.

Amarilis, a young woman whose life had been abruptly and violently cut short, had been an enigma since the discovery of her body. The clues were elusive, the suspects numerous, and the motivations murky. Now, this message hinted at a new piece in this complex puzzle, a key that could shed light on the shadows surrounding her tragic end.

With the arrival of this message, Alfredo found himself at the crossroads of a dilemma. Should he reinsert himself into the vortex of this mystery, deploying once again his sharpness and experience? The calm of Bora-Bora, which he had sought as a refuge, now felt like a golden cage. The call of the mystery was strong, a siren song resonating with the promise of unresolved challenges and truths to be uncovered.

With a sigh mixing resignation and anticipation, Alfredo Montesino knew his Polynesian retirement had come to an end. The story of Amarilis, woven with threads of secrets and silences, was calling him back to the cat-and-mouse game that he so skillfully knew how to play.

III

Amarilis Cintron, the young woman whose tragic fate had moved and puzzled the community, was a figure in life who radiated a unique beauty and vitality. Born in Moca, a town on the charming northwest coast of Puerto Rico, her childhood began in the heart of the region known as Porta del Sol. Moca, a place known for its stunning natural beauty, rich culture, and colorful festivals, was the perfect setting for the beginning of the existence of such a vibrant young woman.

The daughter of humble parents from the fields of the Naranjo neighborhood, in the southeast of the municipality, Amarilis grew up surrounded by a rural environment that shaped her character and her connection with nature. From an early age, her beauty was undeniable: blonde hair that shone under the tropical sun and clear green eyes that reflected the luminosity of the sky and the fields around her.

Running through the fields of Naranjo like a gazelle, Amarilis developed a deep love for nature and outdoor life. Her laughter was like music that mixed with the whisper of the wind among the trees and the song of the birds. This connection with her surroundings not only nourished her soul but also influenced her perspective on life, one where simplicity and natural beauty were more valuable than the artificial adornments of modernity.

As Amarilis grew up, she became a young woman whose presence was like a refreshment for the spirit, a living representation of the grace and charm of her homeland. However, despite her apparent serenity and joy, there were deeper layers to Amarilis, dreams and aspirations that went beyond the confines of her small world in Moca.

The tragedy of her death, the cruel interruption of a life so full of promise and beauty cast a dark shadow over the community that had watched her grow. For those who now sought justice in her name, Amarilis Cintron was not just a victim in a criminal case; she was a reminder of the light and life, cruelly extinguished, but whose story deserved to be told and remembered.

Amarilis, whose early life unfolded among the green fields of Moca, found her path in education at the Gabriela Mistral School, a facility that honored the name of the famous Chilean poet and Nobel Laureate in Literature. From the age of six, Amarilis attended this public school, where her academic trajectory, marked by regular grades, reflected a dedicated young woman, perhaps distracted by dreams that extended beyond the classroom.

Despite not excelling academically, Amarilis had a generous heart and a natural vocation for caring for others. Her interest in medicine stemmed from a deep desire to help and heal, to be a light in the lives of those suffering. However, her grades did not allow her direct entry into a medical program. But, far from being discouraged, she found another route to fulfill her dream of helping people: she became a nurse.

Amarilis entered the nursing school at the medical sciences campus, a path that, although different from what she had initially imagined, offered her the opportunity to be close to patients and make a difference in their lives. In nursing school, her commitment and empathy shone through. Here, Amarilis not only acquired technical skills but also developed a deep understanding of humanity in its most vulnerable moments.

Amarilis's time at the nursing school was a period of personal and professional growth and maturation. In the halls and rooms of this educational center, she learned not only to care for bodies but also to comfort souls, becoming a nurse whose presence was a balm for her patients. Her choice of nursing was not a Plan B, but a manifestation of her true vocation: to be a caregiver, a healer, a light in others' dark moments.

Amarilis's beauty, which emanated from her being like radiant light, was nuanced by her own insecurities. In a culture where pronounced curves were often celebrated and seen as a symbol of attractiveness and femininity, Amarilis felt diminished, conscious of her slimmer, less voluptuous figure. This perception of herself as "flat" at the front and back became a source of unrest and self-consciousness for her, especially during her adolescence, a period marked by changes and new perceptions of body and identity.

Whenever Amarilis stood in front of the full-body mirror, she was confronted by an image that reminded her of how she deviated from the beauty ideals that her culture often idealized. Although her face glowed with green eyes and golden hair, her reflection returned an image that did not meet the expectations of her environment. This internal struggle with her body image was a silent battle, a corner of her life where confidence and self-acceptance waged a constant war against cultural norms and stereotypes.

However, this perception of Amarilis about her own body contrasted with the reality of her impact on those around her. For them, her beauty did not reside in the contours of her figure but in the entirety of her being:

Under his tutelage, Amarilis learned to appreciate nature and find peace in its vast fields. He taught her life lessons through stories of his own youth and the experiences he had accumulated over the years. The wisdom he shared went beyond practical advice; it was wisdom that touched the soul, teaching Amarilis to be strong, resilient, and to stand firm against adversity.

The relationship between Amarilis and her grandfather was special, a deep connection that went beyond the typical grandfather-granddaughter relationship. In his eyes, Amarilis was not just a child to care for, but a kindred spirit, a young soul that resonated with his own understanding of the world. It was this relationship that helped Amarilis become the woman she was empathetic, compassionate, and wise beyond her years, qualities that would later be crucial in her nursing career.

Her grandfather's influence in her life left an indelible mark, shaping not only her personality but also her worldview. Amarilis, despite the challenges she faced, including her insecurities and the absence of her parents, became a quality woman, a living reflection of her grandfather's teachings and love.

Upon completing her nursing education at eighteen, Amarilis faced a critical moment in her life. The recent loss of her grandfather, the central figure in her life and her guide, left a deep mark on her heart. Her grief transformed into a drive to help those who, like her grandfather, were in the final stage of their lives. With this noble goal in mind, Amarilis chose to work in a nursing home, a place where she could make a significant difference.

The island was experiencing a noticeable demographic shift, with an increasingly aging population. Families, facing their own challenges and often overwhelmed by the demands of modern life, found nursing homes a solution for caring for their elderly loved ones. These seniors, many of whom had made significant contributions to society in their youth, now spent their days in these homes, accompanied only by their memories and the occasional visit from family. Their existence, marked by loneliness and forgetfulness, was a grim reality in a world that seemed to have moved on without them.

For Amarilis, each day in the nursing home was an opportunity to provide comfort and joy to these forgotten souls. With empathy born from her own loss, she strived to be a comforting presence in their lives, listening to their stories, meeting their needs, and most importantly, reminding them that they were still valued and loved. In every wrinkled face and in every trembling hand, she saw a reflection of her grandfather, and this inspired her with a passion and dedication that went beyond her professional duties.

Amarilis's work in the nursing home was not only a tribute to her grandfather's memory but also a silent protest against the indifference of a society that too often marginalized its older members. In a world that seemed to have forgotten these elders, Amarilis became a beacon of hope and a reminder that compassion and care still existed. Her work, though often unnoticed, was a form of resistance against loneliness and abandonment, an affirmation of the dignity and inherent value of every stage of human life.

In the medical sciences campus, as Amarilis progressed in her nursing education, her path crossed with that of Julio, a young general surgery resident. Julio, with his enigmatic air and a personality that exuded a mix of charisma and controversy, was embroiled in his own personal storm, battling an identity crisis while navigating the turbulent waters of a relentless surgical residency.

The surgical residency was known for its rigidity and severity, often compared to a concentration camp for its strict structure and excessive expectations. The long hours, constant pressure, and highly competitive environment made it a breeding ground for issues such as drug addiction, alcoholism, and a disturbing rate of suicides among doctors. Amid this environment, Julio was constantly walking a tightrope, struggling not only with the demands of the program but also with his own insecurities and internal doubts.

The arrival of Amarilis in Julio's life was like a ray of light in his darkness. He was instantly captivated by her natural beauty and her aura of serenity, so at odds with the chaos of his daily life. His attraction to her was intense, almost possessive, a flame that ignited a new fire in his heart. This connection, however, came with its share of complications: Julio had a girlfriend whom he loved, but Amarilis's presence left him disoriented, forcing him to reconsider his life and choices.

Amarilis, for her part, found herself unexpectedly in the middle of a love triangle that would challenge her self-perception and place her at the center of passion and conflict she had never sought. The relationship between Amarilis and Julio became a mirror of Julio's internal struggles, reflecting his battle to find his identity and his way in a world that seemed constantly against him.

This new chapter in Amarilis's life led her to an emotional and moral crossroads, where she was forced to weigh Julio's feelings against her own integrity and values. For Amarilis, who had always sought to do good and be a source of care and love, this situation presented a dilemma that went beyond the personal: it was a test of her character and her ability to navigate the complex waters of human relationships.

The encounter between Amarilis and Julio in his apartment marked a turning point in Amarilis's life, a night that left a deep scar, not only physically but also on her psyche. What started with drinks and the carefree use of cannabis quickly turned into an episode of violence and coercion, tearing the fabric of her perception of love and trust. Julio's brutality, an act that crossed all boundaries of respect and consent, left Amarilis in a state of shock and emotional confusion. She spent that night bleeding in pain from her torn virginity.

The young woman from Moca, who had grown up in a loving and caring environment, was now questioning her own understanding of love. Was this the harsh reality of the feeling she had so idealized? Or was it merely a dangerous and destructive fixation? The trauma of the event and the confusion that followed led her to make a difficult but necessary decision: to distance herself from Julio, at least for a while, to reevaluate her life and her feelings.

However, Amarilis's decision to distance herself only served to ignite a spark of aggression in Julio. His obsession with her became more intense, turning his affection into a relentless and suffocating pursuit. The relationship, already tumultuous, turned into a spiral of toxicity, with Julio harassing her incessantly, unable to accept her decision to pull away.

For Amarilis, trapped in this toxic relationship, each day became a challenge to her well-being and her freedom. The girl who once ran freely through the fields of Naranjo, now found herself caught in the vicious cycle of an abusive relationship, struggling to find a way out. This phase of her life was a dark labyrinth of fear, doubt, and danger, a path that led her further away from the joyful and hopeful young woman she once was.

In the midst of Amarilis's internal struggle, one day Julio, with his usual tone of disdain, made a comment that captured the essence of his scorn:

--"You know, Amarilis? I've always been amazed at how someone as 'flat' as you can think they could attract anyone. It's like you're competing in a race without even having legs to run,"-- Julio said, with a mocking smile.

Amarilis, feeling each word as a stab, responded with a mix of sadness and resolve:

--"Julio, my worth is not measured in curves or by others' perceptions. I am learning to love myself as I am, regardless of what you or anyone else might think."--

This exchange of words, loaded with pain and revelation, was a turning point for Amarilis. She was facing not only Julio's hurtful comments but also her own reflection, her insecurities, and the constant struggle to accept her body and her identity. Despite the cruelty of his words, Amarilis began to recognize her own strength and to reject the notion that her value as a person depended on meeting certain physical standards. In her response to

Julio, there was a glimpse of the resilience and dignity she was beginning to claim for herself.

In a setting where beauty was measured in terms of voluptuousness and curves, Amarilis had learned to live with the sensation of not fitting into conventional molds. However, Julio's constant belittling not only attacked her body image but also her worth as a person, making her question her value and identity. These constant attacks left Amarilis in an even more precarious situation. Struggling with the trauma of the assault and Julio's harassment, the hurtful words only served to deepen her pain and confusion. Amidst this emotional turmoil, Amarilis found herself at a crossroads, seeking the strength to reaffirm her identity and value beyond the criticisms and abuse. Her story became one of resistance and rediscovery as she sought to regain the confidence and self-acceptance that Julio and the circumstances of her life had tried to strip away.

Away from Julio's shadow, Amarilis found sanctuary at "Flashes of Light" nursing home, located in Isabela, a town near Moca. This new environment offered her not just an escape from her tumultuous past, but also an opportunity to reconnect with her calling to care for others. In this place, surrounded by life stories and experiences, Amarilis began to heal and regain her sense of identity and purpose.

Social media became an essential tool for Amarilis during this time. It allowed her to maintain a connection with the outside world, preserve her youthful identity, and share aspects of her life that reflected her growing confidence and self-esteem. Through these platforms, she found support, inspiration, and a community that helped her remain steadfast on her path of self-discovery and personal growth.

Over time and thanks to her hard work at the nursing home, Amarilis managed to save enough money to address the physical insecurities that had tormented her for years—the ones Julio had pointed out. She decided to undergo cosmetic surgery to enhance her bust, reduce her waist, and shape her buttocks, procedures she had done at a renowned clinic in the capital. This physical transformation was a significant step for Amarilis in her journey of self-acceptance and empowerment. For her, these changes were not just aesthetic improvements, but acts of personal affirmation, a way to reclaim her body and image as her own.

After the surgery, Amarilis experienced a renewed sense of confidence. She saw herself in a new light, feeling more like the woman she had always wanted to be. Her transformation did not go unnoticed at the nursing home. The residents, always observant of changes in their environment, soon noticed her new appearance. Some of the older men, in a playful and sometimes bold gesture, even pinched her buttocks, surprised and curious about the change.

For Amarilis, these moments were both flattering and a reminder of her new journey of self-acceptance. Despite the hardships she had faced, she was now in a place of greater strength and confidence. However, the external transformation also brought new challenges and perceptions, both of herself and how the world saw her, opening a new chapter in her life full of possibilities but also new realities to navigate.

After her physical transformation, Amarilis's digital presence underwent a noticeable change. Her friends on social media tripled, and with this increase came waves of compliments and admiration. Each new photo she shared was met with a cascade of praises and comments, reflecting the visual impact of her recent change.

However, among this sea of digital admirers, a familiar but unwanted figure lurked: Julio. Taking advantage of the anonymity that social networks offer, he created a profile under a pseudonym, using a caricature as his user icon. With this new disguised identity, he managed to infiltrate Amarilis's virtual circle, going unnoticed among the crowd of followers.

This fake profile allowed Julio to observe and participate in Amarilis's online world undetected. Through comments and reactions, he stayed up to date with her life, maintaining his obsession despite the physical and emotional distance Amarilis had established. For Julio, this profile was a way to keep a connection, albeit one-sided and unknown to Amarilis.

Meanwhile, Amarilis, unaware of Julio's presence in her virtual life, continued to share aspects of her life and transformation. She found in social media a space to express herself and receive the support she had longed for. However, Julio's shadow, although invisible to her, was a reminder that the past still had ways of creeping into her present, reminding her that the echoes of toxic relationships can persist, even in the most unexpected places.

IV

Angel Marcel, a man known in the modern world for his ability to navigate the complexities of love both among those of his own sex and the opposite, also found himself captivated by the presence of Amarilis on social media. Amarilis' photographs, showing her transformation and renewed confidence, did not go unnoticed by Angel, who saw in each digital connection an opportunity for a new encounter, a new game of seduction. Those new sinusoidal curves of the young woman seduced him.

Moved by attraction and curiosity, Angel sent a friend request to Amarilis, a digital gesture that marked the beginning of what he hoped would be a new conquest. For someone with Angel's experience and confidence, Amarilis's quick acceptance was interpreted as a clear sign of interest, an indication that she too was looking for more than just a simple online friendship.

Angel, skilled in the art of digital portrayal, had constructed on social media an image of himself meticulously crafted. His profile presented the narrative of a young entrepreneur, talented and seemingly flawless, a kind of favorite son, the perfect "momma's boy" who had never made a mistake. His ability to weave this illusion was such that even a character as cautious as Little Red Riding Hood might have fallen into his web of deceits.

Amarilis, with her kind nature and an innocence forged from her own experiences of vulnerability, found herself attracted to the idealized image that Angel projected on his profile. The words and images on the screen, carefully selected to paint the perfect picture of a man almost without flaws, impacted her. Angel's virtual wall became a convincing backdrop for his performance, a stage where he could display his charm and charisma.

The virtual connection between Amarilis and Angel, born in the realm of the digital, was based on a carefully constructed perception, one that Angel had meticulously designed. Amarilis, captivated by this portrayal, began to see in Angel someone who could understand her, support her, and possibly offer her a new chance at love and human connection.

However, behind this connection lay the truth that Angel was not completely what he seemed. His online character was a façade, a mask cleverly created to attract and captivate. For Amarilis, the revelation of this reality could be a new blow to her confidence and perception, another test in her journey to find authenticity in a world often full of illusions.

Amarilis, for her part, accepted Angel's friend request without giving it too much importance, although she was impressed by what she read about him. For her, social media was a platform to connect with the world, to share her story and her experiences, without hidden intentions or expectations of romantic encounters. However, the interpretation that Angel made of her acceptance revealed the differences in their perspectives and expectations.

With innate charm and an attractive presence, Angel soon started a conversation with Amarilis. For him, each interaction was a step in the game of seduction, an art at which he had become expert. In his mind, Amarilis had already entered his orbit; a new interest that aroused his curiosity and desire.

What Angel did not know was that Amarilis was at a point in her life where the search for meaning and genuine connection went beyond simple physical attraction or superficial games. Amarilis's evolution, marked by difficult experiences and a process of self-acceptance, had led her to value deeper aspects of human relationships.

Thus, while Angel saw in Amarilis a potential adventure, she, in her journey of self-discovery and growth, might find herself looking for something beyond what Angel was accustomed to offering. The interaction between these two characters promised to be a complex dance of intentions and discoveries, another chapter in the story of Amarilis, where her choices and reactions would continue to define her path and her identity.

In the vast universe of social media, existence becomes a kind of illusion, a distorted reflection projected through the bright screens of our contemporary communication devices. People become architects of a mirage, building images of themselves as culinary masters, insatiable travelers, exceptionally enlightened beings, in an exhibition of happiness and success that often borders on the absurd. These presentations, which more resemble a parade of vanities than a portrait of reality, are both puzzling and somewhat terrifying.

Truthfulness is constantly called into question, distorted by the carefully selected and edited photos and videos that flood these platforms. Reality, as if elusive, hides behind filters and flattering angles. The comments, riddled with spelling and logical errors, sometimes make one question the authenticity of the education proclaimed by their authors. It is a dance of masks and appearances, a theater where millions perform their happiness in contrast to the possible unhappiness of their real lives.

In this world of digital mirages, was Angel, a character of complex duality. As an emotional and sexual chameleon, his ability to love both men and women with equal fervor made him an ambiguous figure on the sexuality spectrum. However, this flexibility was accompanied by a tendency to devalue his current partner depending on the company he kept at the time. Angel, in his quest for affection and validation, navigated a sea of changing emotions and desires, where his identity seemed as fluid as the waters of an unpredictable river.

Thus, in a world where authenticity is often sacrificed on the altar of appearance, Angel moved like a seasoned actor, playing different roles depending on the audience before him. In the land of projected shadows and half-truths of social media, Angel was both a victim and a perpetrator of this grand deception, a being in constant struggle with his own identity on a stage where reality and fiction are inextricably intertwined.

Unintimidated by the distances imposed by the virtual, Angel embarked on a strategy to approach Amarilis through social media. Becoming a constant admirer, his goal was to weave a network of flattery and comments, creating a bridge that would allow him to cross from the digital world to the real one. The subtlety of his words and the frequency of his interactions were designed to attract her, to turn curiosity into interest, and interest into something more tangible.

In the digital age, where identities are often constructed and reconstructed behind screens, Angel was aware of the blurry line between reality and fiction. The Amarilis he knew through social media could be an illusion, a carefully crafted creation, as real as an artificial intelligence designed to mimic life. With "influencers" and online personalities often sculpting alternate realities, Angel could not be sure of the authenticity of the young woman who had captured his interest.

Eager to confirm whether the Amarilis he had come to admire was really flesh and blood, Angel made a bold decision. Guided by the scattered clues in her posts, which revealed her workplace in Isabela, he planned a surprise visit. For him, this was the only way to verify the reality of Amarilis, to understand if the woman who appeared on social media was the same one who breathed and lived in the real world.

His journey to Isabela was filled with anticipation and curiosity. Amarilis, for her part, unaware of Angel's intentions, continued her routine in the nursing home, a refuge where she had found peace and purpose. The potential disruption of Angel into her real life promised to be an encounter between two worlds: that of digital projections and that of tangible existence, a clash between what is perceived and what really is. This next step in their story was laden with unknowns and possibilities, in a game of reality and perception where each had their own expectations and secrets.

Angel arrived at 'Flashes of Light' in Isabela, a place where hope and care intertwined in the lives of its residents. With slight hesitation, he pressed the entrance buzzer, an act that marked the crossing of both a physical and emotional threshold. The door was answered by the receptionist, a woman with an imposing presence whose robust figure and determined attitude gave her an air more befitting a nightclub bouncer than a nursing home attendant.

--"You!... What are you looking for here?"-- she asked, her voice resonating with authority.

Angel, taken aback and with a mix of nervousness and anticipation, replied.

--"Does Miss Amarilis Cintron work here?"--

The receptionist, maintaining her stern expression, probed further:

--"Who is looking for her, if I may ask?"--

--"Angel Marcel, at your service. I know her from social media,"-- he stammered, his initial confidence fading under the woman's scrutinizing gaze.

--"Wait here, for now,"-- she replied firmly. As she closed the door in front of Angel, it was clear from her demeanor that she considered the possibility that this unexpected visitor could be a threat, a potential danger to the residents of the home. The safety of those under her care was her priority, and she would not allow a stranger, emerging out of nowhere with such a vague story, to just walk in.

Angel stood there, processing the exchange, with the door closed between him and the object of his search. His journey to 'Flashes of Light' had begun with an unexpected obstacle, one that made him question his decision to seek out Amarilis in the real world, beyond the filter of social media.

When Amarilis Cintron appeared, her presence illuminated the space, a stark contrast to the scene that had unfolded so far. Dressed in her nurse's uniform, white and without a cap, her beauty was undeniable and even more striking in person than in the images from social media.

"Hello! I'm Amarilis Cintron, were you looking for me?" she asked with a voice that mixed curiosity and caution.

Angel, surprised and visibly impressed, could barely hide his astonishment. His eyes widened, taking in every detail of the woman before him. The Amarilis he now saw was the embodiment of the image he had cherished in his mind: blonde hair framing a face with clear eyes, a figure enhanced by the transformation she had chosen. The contrast between the Amarilis he knew from the screen and the real woman before him was striking, and at that moment, Angel realized he had underestimated the impact she would have on him.

Angel's reaction did not go unnoticed by Amarilis, who was used to a certain level of attention since her transformation. However, Angel's gaze told her that there was something more in his interest, something beyond mere physical admiration. At that moment, a silent exchange began between them, filled with possibilities and unanswered questions, marking the start of a new phase in both of their lives.

Amarilis, demonstrating her usual hospitality, led Angel to the nursing home's living room, a spacious area furnished with comfortable armchairs, most of which were occupied by the residents. It measured thirty by sixteen feet. The atmosphere was permeated with a mix of characteristic smells: the unmistakable scent of old age, octogenarian sweat glands, and mothballs, mixed with the more pungent odor of physical frailty. Amidst this mosaic of aromas, Amarilis's French perfume stood out as a distinct and fresh note.

The residents of the home, each immersed in their own world, distant and disconnected from the surrounding reality, cast glances at Angel that ranged from curiosity to suspicion. Among them, some with the mischief born from years of wisdom, looked at Angel with interest, almost as if they sensed he was more than just a simple visitor, perhaps even the boyfriend of the young and attractive nurse.

The large and prominent television, a sixty-five-inch screen, broadcasted the midday news at a moderate volume but seemed to capture no one's interest. Instead, the residents' gazes were fixed on Angel, a new and unfamiliar face that disrupted the monotony of their daily routine. At that moment, Angel became the center of attention, a focal point in the quiet existence of the nursing home.

For his part, Angel was almost taken aback, almost thinking he had arrived in heaven. For a brief moment, his mind wandered to his late grandfather. But he was disoriented, seeing all these old folks who in turn were looking at him, some drooling from the corner of their mouths, their saliva thick and slow-moving. Exactly what he would become over time without anyone's help. -- "These are my patients,"-- Amarilis commented proudly as she introduced them one by one by their name or as they had chosen to call themselves upon entering the nursing home. Some had even changed their names, dissatisfied with the ones they were given naturally. You know how old people are, there's no contradicting them.

In those lost gazes were Amarilis, Angel, and the bunch of old folks from the nursing home when the imposing initial bearer, large and fat with a commanding voice, imperiously ordered: --"Let's go to lunch...time to eat...move to the dining room,"-- there was not even a please, just a curt notification that had to be obeyed. And so, the encampment that stayed overnight did. Slowly, with clumsiness and uncertainty, the nursing home's troop moved little by little, some shuffling in their walkers to a room adjacent to the left that had a long rectangular table with space for about twenty diners. Several in wheelchairs had to be pushed to the dining table. The large woman and Amarilis took care of these last ones. Angel was not invited to eat. They served salad, mashed potatoes, and shredded chicken in red sauce. One or two complained since the menus are the same, just rotated weekly. It must not be forgotten that at that age one is, as they say, unhooked. Those who had stomach tubes for feeding also connected, as at that age or condition they could not chew, swallow, or both.

Angel, finding himself in an environment so different from what he was accustomed to, became a silent observer of the nursing home's routine. The living room, a stage where the daily care of the elderly unfolded, was revealed to him as a human tragicomedy, full of both bitter and sweet moments. He, unfamiliar with this world, did not actively participate, choosing instead to remain a distant spectator, watching attentively but not getting involved.

This passivity of Angel, his choice not to offer help or interact with the residents, might have been due to a mix of uncertainty and respect, or perhaps a lack of understanding of how to insert himself into an environment so alien to him. His gaze was that of a student, someone who analyzes and processes what he sees, trying to understand a reality that was completely new and unknown to him.

For Amarilis, this was her everyday life, a balance between care and empathy, sadness, and joy. She moved with a familiarity and purpose that contrasted with Angel's immobility. In this contrast, two different worlds were drawn together in that space: Amarilis's world, marked by dedication and service, and Angel's world, defined by observation and calculation.

This interaction, or the lack of it, between Angel and the nursing home environment, as well as his focus on Amarilis, painted a picture of a man still in the process of discovering how to relate not only to her but also to an aspect of life that was foreign to him. In this experience, Angel not only faced the challenge of approaching Amarilis but also of understanding and appreciating the depth and complexity of her world.

Angel's unexpected appearance at the nursing home, especially during such a critical time as lunch, reflected his unfamiliarity with the routines and sensitivities of the place. By not having arranged a prior appointment with Amarilis, his arrival was not only untimely but also placed him in the role of a mere observer during an intimate moment of the day for the residents.

Lunch at a nursing home is not just a meal; it is a daily event filled with interactions and established routines, a time for both physical and social nourishment. Angel's arrival during this time offered him a unique window into life at the nursing home, allowing him to see the residents and staff, including Amarilis, in their natural environment.

For Amarilis, this was a time to focus on her responsibilities, to ensure that each resident received the necessary attention and care. Angel's presence, though unexpected, did not alter her commitment to her job. For her, the residents were her priority, and any visit, planned or not, took a back seat to her duties.

Angel, witnessing this dynamic, might have gained a new appreciation for Amarilis's dedication and commitment. Observing from the sidelines, he could have noticed the care and respect with which she treated each of the residents, an aspect of her personality that might not have been evident through their interactions on social media.

This meeting, although it did not result in the direct and personal interaction Angel might have hoped for, was an opportunity for him to better understand Amarilis's world and the environment in which she chose to spend her days. For Amarilis, it was a reminder that despite her life on social media, her reality was deeply rooted in the nursing home and in the care of those who depended on her.

An hour after the nursing home staff finished feeding their clients, Amarilis returned to attend to her unexpected visitor.

--"Now that we've finished giving lunch to the patients, how can I help you?"-- Amarilis asked, her voice imbued with a professionalism that betrayed no hint of her internal surprise at seeing Angel in person. The moment her eyes landed on him; she couldn't help but notice his attractiveness. Angel, with his tousled dark hair and olive-colored eyes, looked as if he had stepped out of a Hellenic legend, a modern Apollo who had mistakenly wandered into the mundane realm of the nursing home.

At first glance, one could easily imagine that Amarilis and Angel would make a perfect couple, like figures from an idealized romance. Two double A's. However, as is well known, appearances can be deceiving, and external beauty is rarely a reliable indicator of compatibility between two souls. Aware of this, Amarilis maintained her professionalism, waiting to understand the purpose of Angel's unexpected visit.

--"Well, I just wanted to make sure you were real, you know, there's so much fiction on the networks," he hesitated.

--"Did you come all this way just to tell me that?"-- she reproached him.

--"Not from very far, I live in the town of Captain Correa, Arecibo."--

--"Ah, well, that's quite close. I am from Moca and still live in Moca,"-- she continued. – "I'm very close to my parents' house."--

--"Do you still live with them?"-- he asked, his tone carrying a hint of a romantic inquisitor, as if trying to decipher whether what he had in front of him was a princess waiting to be rescued.

--"Yes,"-- Amarilis lamented, her response brief yet loaded with a subtle emotionality that revealed the complexity underlying her simple statement.

And so, the young people continued their exchange of questions without promiscuity until Amarilis was forced to interrupt the conversation, explaining that she had work commitments. Angel, understanding the situation, politely said goodbye, but not before asking for her phone number. To this, Amarilis explained that it was her policy not to share her number with someone she had just met. For the young man, winning Amarilis's heart was proving to be no easy challenge.

Angel was left with the only viable option: to continue using digital platforms to try to arrange a meeting with Amarilis.

V

That evening, Amarilis returned to her parents' house, radiant after her encounter with Angel. He was a handsome young man who had shown his patience by waiting for her while she attended to the elderly in the nursing home during lunch. Following a past, turbulent relationship with Julio, which had left scars more than a year ago, she was worried about the idea of opening up to a new relationship. However, Angel stirred in her a different feeling, a kind of hope. When her parents asked about her day, with the honesty that characterized her, she shared that she had met a boy and, driven by a surge of confidence, had given him her address in Moca so he could visit her when they arranged it.

In that environment of shadows and memories, Leo, the pseudonym chosen by Julio—the spurned lover and ghostly figure from Amarilis's most turbulent days— delved into the digital ocean hoping to catch, even from a distance, the virtual traces of Amarilis. Amarilis's aesthetic transformation had only intensified Leo's desire and obsession to win back what he considered the epitome of femininity and beauty, a treasure he had lost but was determined to reclaim. This fixation was nothing but the bitter fruit of a year's absence, a period during which Julio's life had plummeted, thrusting him into a chasm of despair and idleness.

Since that misfortune which stripped him of his career and Amarilis, his existence had turned into a barren wasteland. Stripped of his dreams and exiled from the promising future he once envisioned, Julio, now under the alias of Leo, wandered aimlessly, caught in an existential limbo fueled by the remnants of paternal generosity and the involuntary refuge in his grandmother's home. This last sanctuary, an oasis in his personal desert, provided the essentials for survival: food, a roof to shelter under, and a modest allowance that barely covered the gasoline, the vital minimum that allowed him to keep moving, albeit aimlessly.

In this purgatory of his existence, the figure of Amarilis shone like a distant beacon, the only certainty in a sea of uncertainties. His forced exile from the medical world, the result of those unspeakable acts that had led to professional ruin, had turned into a life sentence from which he saw no escape. However, in his mind, he plotted, devising plans and strategies with the vain hope of redemption or, at least, of a sweet revenge that might give some meaning to his wilted existence.

The dismissal from his medical residency, a blow from which he never recovered, had branded him with the stigma of irremediable failure. Now, secluded in the safe but stifling space of his grandmother's house, Julio, transformed into Leo for the virtual world, clung to the only obsession left: the conquest of Amarilis, that elusive muse who, since her transformation, seemed more unreachable than ever. In this personal crusade, reality and fiction intertwined in a macabre dance where love, desire, and obsession swirled on the edge of the abyss.

After his former classmates had graduated, Julio decided to visit Lionel, who had achieved the distinction of general surgeon. Lionel, not without some pride, showed Julio the diploma he had earned, a recognition for completing his general surgery training awarded by the academic institution. Julio's situation evoked a sense of pity in Lionel. In a moment of carelessness, when Lionel went to freshen up, Julio found himself alone with the valuable document. This pause provided the perfect opportunity to take a photograph of the diploma with his sophisticated mobile phone, equipped with a three-camera system. Although he had toyed with the idea without deciding, the temptation to create a copy of the diploma by changing the name to his own suddenly seemed feasible. After all, he had completed almost all of his residency and possessed the necessary knowledge for managing patients in a surgical setting. Julio began to envision a plan: he would open a clinic in some remote corner of the island devoid of general surgeons, where he could perform minor procedures. This would introduce a significant income to his otherwise stagnant financial situation.

In the intricate labyrinth of his life, Julio had crossed the Rubicon of morality by replicating his former classmate's diploma, printing his own name with a precision that bordered on artistic perfection. He was now the holder of a forged credential, a mirage of achievement that shone with the false promise of competence and integrity. This feat of deception marked the beginning of a darker and more dangerous journey in Julio's life.

With the scheme completed, the next step required similar cunning: finding a discreet corner to set up his sanctuary of operations, a place remote enough to avoid scrutiny but accessible to those thirsty for eternal beauty and youth. In this search, Julio envisioned a modest clinic, a temple dedicated to vanity, where he could practice his newly acquired 'profession' without raising suspicions.

Aware that his charade needed an additional veneer of credibility, Julio immersed himself in the vast ocean of knowledge available on the internet, enrolling in cosmetic surgery courses that promised certifications with minimal effort. These new 'academic achievements' would be the jewels in the crown of his deceit, tools designed to seduce those unhappy with their reflection in the mirror, seeking transformation at the hands of someone they believed to be an expert.

In Julio's mind, his venture was not an act of villainy, but rather a philosophical service; a cure for the modern discontent with one's image. He saw his future patients not as victims, but as souls in search of aesthetic redemption, willing to pay the price for an illusion of perfection. "After all," he thought, "anyone seeking to alter their appearance is already living a deception, perpetually wandering in a desire for metamorphosis."

Thus, armed with his forged diploma and a growing collection of dubious certificates, Julio was preparing to launch into the beauty market, ready to exploit the eternal human quest for youth and physical perfection. In this dangerous game of mirrors and smoke, Julio, or rather, 'Dr. Leo', as he now preferred to be called, was about to embark on an adventure that would blur the lines even further between truth and fiction, between the healer and the charlatan. In his surgical theatre, every incision would be a verse in the poetry of his grand illusion, each suture a stroke on the canvas of his legend built on lies and half-truths.

Julio, in his labyrinth of arrogance and misapplied intelligence, had become a master of deception, a character who defied norms with reckless audacity. He saw his expulsion from the surgical residency not as a lesson in humility, but as a temporary setback on his path to greatness. His ego, inflated to the point of bursting, blinded him to any glimmer of self-criticism or reflection. In his mind, he had constructed an alternate reality where his dismissal was merely a misjudgment by those unable to recognize his genius.

Armed with forgeries and a master plan, Julio embarked on a new chapter of his life, one in which he would reinvent himself as a renowned cosmetic surgeon. This was not merely a whim, but a declaration of power, a means to prove to everyone, especially to Amarilis, his supposed superiority and worth. In his delusion of grandeur, he imagined a future where, through his success as a fake surgeon, Amarilis would come back to him, regretful and admiring, surrendering to the idol he believed himself to be. The possessiveness he felt towards Amarilis reflected his narcissism, an extension of his need for control and admiration.

Julio did not see Amarilis for who she really was, but rather as a trophy to be claimed, a symbol of his dominance and success. In his distorted mind, Amarilis had no will or desires of her own; she was merely another piece on the chessboard of his life, destined to be captured. Julio's obsession with winning her back was not based on love, but on selfish affirmation, on the need to prove to himself that he could have everything he wanted, even by manipulating reality to his liking.

This path that Julio chose, paved with falsehoods and delusions of grandeur, placed him on a dangerous trajectory, not just for himself but for those who crossed his path. His refusal to face the consequences of his actions and his inability to recognize his mistakes had led him to a point of no return, where the line between right and wrong had faded in pursuit of his unbridled ambitions.

Julio delved into the realm of aesthetics with a dedication that bordered on obsession, devouring every superficial course he found on techniques for rejuvenating and beautifying: from eyelid lifts to the insertion of tension threads to correct time-marked faces. He absorbed knowledge on how to inject various substances to sculpt facial contours, eyebrows, and lips, seeking the ideal of perfection that modern society so craved. In a vanity-driven act, he became his own guinea pig, experimenting with these "youth elixirs" to ensure he presented a flawless image in front of his future patients.

Choosing Jayuya as the stage for his grand act, Julio established his clinic in this quiet town, far from the scrutinizing eyes of the big cities. He hired a nurse with legitimate credentials, set up a modest operating room in an adjoining room, and acquired an arsenal of medicines and anesthetics, including a pulse monitor and an oximeter to monitor his patients' vitality during procedures. Shielded by the shadow of his legitimate medical diploma, complemented by the forged general surgery diploma and a series of aesthetic certificates, he faced no significant obstacles in obtaining the necessary license to administer controlled substances, presenting himself to the world as a generalist with a cosmetic twist.

Thus, Julio positioned himself as the self-proclaimed pioneer of cosmetic surgery in the heart of the island, ready to dazzle and transform those seeking his art. But his confidence was not solely based on the knowledge acquired through traditional channels; he also turned to the vast digital universe, from video platform tutorials to consultations with the always available, albeit questionable, artificial intelligence. This AI, despite its name, was a cold, calculating resource, devoid of human warmth and understanding, but in Julio's hands, it became just another tool to perfect his technique.

In this scenario, Julio, under the guise of professionalism and excellence, hid the reality of his training and ethics, a construct as artificial as the results he promised his patients. His clinic, though outwardly equipped and ready to meet the region's beauty needs, was the perfect setting for an impending tragedy, where the line between well-being and risk was increasingly blurred, held only by the fragile thread of aspirations and deceit.

Through social media, and with noticeable changes in his facial expression—results of cosmetic procedures he had practiced on himself, some even under local anesthesia—Julio, now under the pseudonym Leo, managed to capture Amarilis's attention, his ex-girlfriend. He was practically unrecognizable. Embodying his new alter ego, Leo constantly tried to show Amarilis the growing prestige he was gaining as a pioneer in the field of modern aesthetics. He dreamed of having her by his side, working together in this new venture, and was willing to offer her more than she earned at the nursing home to persuade her. In his twisted mind, it was the best option for a nurse and companion of passion. All this unfolding fraud would be mitigated with a trustworthy person who believed in him. However, Amarilis, true to the promise made to her grandfather before his departure from this world, chose to stay at the nursing home, finding there not just a job but a vocation and a purpose that went beyond any material offering. Despite this, Leo would not give up so easily and continued to plan new strategies to convince her, displaying a tenacity that bordered on obsession. His persistence knew no bounds, and he was prepared to do whatever it took to have her by his side, disregarding Amarilis's wishes, and autonomy in his effort to win her back.

Leo, despite the transformations he had inflicted on himself, still retained the essence of who he had been as Julio. The more defined eyelids, enhanced cheekbones, voluminous lips, and pronounced chin gave him a new visage, a significant change complemented by a thick, artificially darkened beard—a stark contrast to his natural color—making him unrecognizable even to those with whom he had shared years of medical training. However, beneath this revamped exterior, his voice, his egocentrism, and a barely concealed malice remained unchanged.

In his rare encounters with former colleagues who struggled to recognize him, Leo adopted an air of distinction and fabricated achievements. --"Did you finish your surgical residency?"-- they would ask, to which he, with a barely perceptible smile, replied: --"Yes, in the United States, with additional training in aesthetics."-- His lies flowed with astonishing ease, each word another brick in the wall of his new identity.

All this effort, this meticulous and calculated change, had one sole purpose: to win back Amarilis, the girl he had deflowered and who had become the obsession of his life, an obsession he needed to reclaim at all costs. In the solitude of his room, facing the mirror that reflected a man he no longer recognized as himself, Leo pondered his plan, his determination growing with every thought.

"You're either mine or no one's," he murmured to himself, the phrase echoing in the room like a dark mantra. This fixed and obsessive idea was the fuel of his existence. No matter the cost of his transformation or the lies he had to spin to maintain his façade; Amarilis was the prize, the ultimate goal that justified all means.

In these moments of introspection, Leo did not see the ethical boundaries he was crossing nor the lives, including his own, he was willing to jeopardize. He saw only the object of his desire, an obsession that consumed him and dictated each of his actions, blinding him to the reality that Amarilis, with her strength and dedication to others, was beyond his reach, beyond the power of his manipulations. Yet, he persisted, unable to accept that some things, once lost, are irretrievable, and that true love cannot be forced or won back through deceit and obsession.

Digging deeper into the complex web of Julio's life, we can unravel why he chose to change his name to Leo. It was not hard to understand the transition; his first two names were Julio Leonardo. Thus, by adopting the name "Leo," he wasn't breaking any certification laws nor straying too far from his original identity. This alias, in addition to giving him a fresh start, provided an extra layer of separation from his troubled past. The clinic, which would come to be known as Dr. Leo's office, would become his sanctuary and stage, a place where he could reinvent himself.

He wanted to be addressed informally, seeking to create an artificial closeness with his patients, a way to erase traditional doctor-patient barriers and foster a sense of trust, albeit superficial. Initially, his office remained empty, a silent echo of his unchecked ambition. However, over time, those unfortunates enough to seek more affordable alternatives to the expensive services in the capital found his clinic a viable option. Located in the heart of the island, it offered convenience and reduced prices, attracting a clientele willing to overlook certain standards in favor of accessibility and proximity.

Initially, Leo faced the typical complications one might expect in any medical practice. However, he was about to encounter a challenge that would exceed anything he had anticipated. This challenge would test not only his skills as a doctor but also threaten to expose the fragile façade he had so painstakingly constructed. Life, as it often does, had prepared a lesson for Leo that went beyond the professional, one that would force him to confront the consequences of his choices, his ethics, and the true cost of his boundless ambition.

VI

Alfredo Montesino, still wrapped in the golden glow of his Polynesian tan, marked a stark contrast with the grayness of the days on the island where he had grown up. He soon contacted Agent Prieto, driven by a mix of professional curiosity and personal unease that had grown during his time away from home. His money was running out. The call was direct, no beating around the bush, typical of someone used to dealing with the complexity of human enigmas.

--"Ernesto, I'm back. I need to know what has happened with Amarilis's case,"-- said Alfredo, his voice still carrying the echo of the Pacific waves.

Agent Prieto, for his part, felt a renewed sense of urgency upon hearing Montesino's voice. He knew that Alfredo had a unique talent for unraveling mysteries that eluded others.

--"Alfredo, I'm glad you called. This case... it's turned into a dead end. The command has already put it on the cold case list, and resources are being reassigned."--

--"Then, it's time for us to step in,"-- Montesino replied with determination. The news of a reward offered by Amarilis's parents, a desperate gesture to find justice for their daughter, only added extra weight to his decision. Maybe he could go back to Bora-Bora. Alfredo was no stranger to the desperation of those seeking answers; he had seen it too many times.

--"I'm going to need access to all the case files, Ernesto. Every interview, every crime scene report, every piece of evidence collected. And I want to speak with Amarilis's parents personally,"-- insisted Alfredo, his mind already tracing potential paths through the labyrinth of evidence and testimonies.

Agent Prieto nodded, though Alfredo couldn't see it. --"I'll get you what you need. You know I trust your judgment, Alfredo. If anyone can make sense of this mess, it's you."--

With that conversation, Alfredo Montesino was diving back into the turbulent waters of criminal investigation, carrying with him the hope of those left behind by the system. The case of Amarilis would not be forgotten, not as long as he could do something about it. As he hung up the phone, Alfredo felt the tan from his vacation beginning to fade against the grim reality he was about to face. But he was ready; after all, unraveling hidden truths was his true calling.

Alfredo Montesino listened attentively to Amarilis's parents as they guided him through the farm, an oasis of memories and pain in the heart of Moca. The room of "the baby girl", preserved as a shrine to her memory, was a silent testimony to the tragedy that had struck them. Each object, each photograph, spoke of the life Amarilis had lived, of her dreams, her achievements, and the abrupt turns her fate had taken.

The parents shared with Alfredo the stories of her childhood, her passion for nursing, and the heartbreak that had left her devastated, a painful chapter in her life that had remained hidden behind her smile. They told him about her dedication to the nursing home in Isabela, how, seeking a new beginning, Amarilis had decided to undergo some cosmetic procedures, and about the appearance of a young man who had visited her and asked her out, lighting up her days with the promise of new beginnings.

But it was the mention of a doctor, who had offered her a position at a cosmetic clinic, that caught Alfredo's attention. This information, vague in the grief-stricken parents' memories, could be key to understanding the events that led to Amarilis's tragic end. However, the uncertainty over whether Amarilis had accepted or rejected the offer, or if she was still considering it, raised more questions than answers.

The handing over of Amarilis's social media keys to Alfredo was an act of trust and desperation by the bereaved parents. Armed with this access, Alfredo knew he had a new door to open in the investigation, a digital path to explore for clues that had remained hidden.

Back at his office, Alfredo delved into Amarilis's online world, navigating through her posts, interactions, and private messages that might reveal the network of relationships and events that culminated in her murder. It was meticulous work, each click a potential revelation, each message a possible clue.

Among the lights and shadows of Amarilis's digital life, Alfredo sought answers, sought justice. The story of Amarilis, woven through her words and those of her acquaintances, unfolded before him, promising to unveil the secrets that had led to her unexpected and tragic end. It was a difficult path, filled with hopes and disappointments, but Alfredo was determined to follow it to the end, for Amarilis and for those who, still engulfed in sorrow, awaited peace in the truth.

With the police file in his hands, Alfredo Montesino delved into the details of Amarilis's case with the meticulousness of an expert and the empathy of someone who understands the human pain behind the cold reports. The photos of Amarilis at the crime scene displayed the brutality of her end, while the post-mortem reports revealed the surgical precision with which the final act that took her life was carried out.

The detailed description of the autopsy indicated that Amarilis's throat had been cut with a precise incision between the second and third tracheal cartilages, a technique identical to that used in a tracheotomy, but without damaging the adjacent blood vessels. This particular detail resonated with a sinister echo in Alfredo's mind, suggesting the hand of someone with advanced medical knowledge. The cause of death, asphyxiation, and hypoxia, pointed to a prolonged agony, an undeserved end for any human being.

The finding of semen in both cavities suggests a despicable post-mortem act, adding an additional layer of violence and dehumanization to the already gruesome murder. The fact that there was no evidence of a struggle could indicate that Amarilis was taken by surprise or somehow incapacitated before her death.

The report continued to state that the semen found did not match any profile in the police database, indicating that the killer had no recorded history of sexual crimes, or at least had not been caught for them. This dead-end in forensic evidence only served to deepen the mystery surrounding the case.

Piecing together the puzzle, Alfredo couldn't help but feel a renewed sense of urgency. The methodical nature of Amarilis's murder, combined with the violence exerted upon her, painted a grim picture of premeditation and cruelty. The precision of the cut made on Amarilis's trachea pointed to someone with anatomical or surgical knowledge, which led Alfredo to consider the possibility that the killer might be connected in some way to the medical field.

Reflecting on this new line of inquiry, Alfredo knew he had to proceed with caution. Every step had to be measured, every lead followed meticulously. It was clear he was looking for someone who not only possessed a cold, calculating mind but also had the skill and knowledge to execute a murder so meticulously. Armed with this new understanding, Alfredo prepared to dive even deeper into the abyss, determined to uncover the monster behind the mask of knowledge and sanity.

Alfredo Montesino faces a complicated dilemma. There weren't many suspects, but identifying and proving who had perpetrated Amarilis's murder became the central focus of his investigation. He mentally reviewed the elements at his disposal: a young man driving a Ford

Bronco with tinted windows, a body lacking scratches that would indicate a struggle, the murderer's genetic material that found no match in the databases, and social media communications from two individuals, Angel and Dr. Leo, the latter linked to a cosmetic clinic.

The Ford Bronco, which could have served as a crucial clue immediately after the crime, now represented a dead end. Too much time had passed; the vehicle could easily have been discarded, sold, or even altered to avoid recognition.

The genetic material, on the other hand, was a solid piece of evidence but without a known owner. With no matches in the police DNA bank, this lead also cooled off. Science, as advanced as it was, couldn't conjure a name from nothing.

VII

Angel, after visiting Amarilis's parents' home in Moca, had built an image of a young man who was interested and respectful. The dates with Amarilis, marked by the courtesy of bringing her back before midnight, had left a positive impression on her parents and the community. It was clear that Amarilis valued her work at the nursing home and that Angel deeply respected that commitment.

The news of Amarilis's murder struck Angel like a sudden blow, plunging him into deep depression. Confusion and sorrow enveloped him, unable to comprehend how a being so full of light and dedication as Amarilis could have been taken from this world so brutally. The pain he felt was a reflection not only of the loss of what Amarilis represented but also of the possibility of a future that would never materialize.

In his mourning, Angel returned to Amarilis's parents' house, a gesture of solidarity and respect towards the bereaved family. He had already paid his respects at the funeral home, where Amarilis's body was laid out in an atmosphere of wrenching grief and nostalgia. The procession to the municipal cemetery, where she was given a Christian burial, was a farewell act not just for family and friends but also for Angel, who saw in that final moment a closure to the brief but meaningful connection he had had with Amarilis.

This act of Angel's, returning to Amarilis's parents' house after the funeral, was both an attempt to find comfort and to offer it. He was seeking answers, though deep down he knew some questions would forever remain unanswered. His presence in the house was a silent testament to the impact Amarilis had made on his life, even though their acquaintance had been short.

The emerging relationship between Amarilis and Angel was a window into what might have been, a promise of the future cut short by tragedy. In the short time that Amarilis got to know Angel, she began to see the world and relationships in a different light. Angel's thoughtful and respectful actions were a balm to Amarilis's past wounds, showing that love, based on mutual respect and consideration, was possible.

The tenderness with which Angel treated Amarilis, from simple gestures like holding her hand during a walk, kissing her gently, or showing courtesy by opening the car door for her, were living proof that not all men are the same. Amarilis, whose past experiences had shaped a cautious view of love and relationships, found in Angel a reason to reconsider these beliefs. He, consciously or not, was rebuilding Amarilis's trust in love, showing her that passion and respect can coexist harmoniously in a healthy relationship.

Perhaps, if fate had been different, their relationship might have blossomed into something deeper, possibly even a family. The potential of their bond, full of promise and hope, makes the loss of Amarilis even more heartbreaking. Life, with its inherent unpredictability, is often disrupted by events beyond our control, whether due to illness, the inexorable passage of time, or, in the most tragic and abrupt cases, acts of violence that snatch loved ones from our side.

While Amarilis was exploring the budding connection with Angel, Leo, using his digital cunning, was infiltrating Amarilis's life through social media. His interest in her was not casual; Amarilis, being a nurse and having resorted to cosmetic surgery to alter her figure—a detail that did not go unnoticed in the virtual realm—became a target for his insinuations and advances.

The transformation of Amarilis did not go unnoticed by Leo, who, under his new identity, watched from a distance the changes she had chosen for herself. These changes, which made her look the way she had always wanted, were a constant reminder to Leo, formerly known as Julio, of his enduring influence on her life, albeit in an indirect and unrecognized way.

Leo's perception of his role in Amarilis's decision to undergo aesthetic procedures was complex. On one hand, he felt flattered, interpreting Amarilis's changes as a validation of his past insinuations and criticisms about her appearance. This distorted perception filled him with a misguided sense of pride and satisfaction, believing he had been the catalyst for her transformation.

On the other hand, this flattery was intertwined with a sense of ownership; Leo saw Amarilis's change as an opportunity to reclaim her, to make her "his" in a way he had not managed before. This possessive and obsessive mindset revealed the depth of his egocentrism and his inability to recognize Amarilis as an autonomous person with her own desires and decisions, independent of his influence.

In his mind, Leo justified his previous insinuations and manipulations as beneficial, ignoring the pain and insecurity his actions had caused Amarilis. This self-deception allowed him to see his obsession not as an act of control or abuse, but as a kind of entitled right over Amarilis, based on the influence he believed he had over her.

This complex web of pride, ownership, and justification in Leo's mind became the driving force behind his actions. Armed with this distorted justification, Leo was preparing to act, determined to reinsert himself into Amarilis's life with a renewed sense of ownership and determination.

Amidst the crisis, the real shortcomings of Dr. Leo's makeshift medical practice came to light. Without the proper credentials or the requisite surgical acumen, he found himself floundering, desperately trying to manage a situation that was rapidly spiraling out of control. The operating room, which had been a stage for his grandiose delusions of competence, suddenly became a stark tableau of his inadequacies.

In a frantic effort to save his patient and salvage what he could of his crumbling facade, Leo attempted an emergency procedure. His hands, though steady in deceit, trembled with the realization of his own limitations. The woman lay unconscious, her life hanging by a thread as Leo navigated through his inadequacies, compounded by his lack of real surgical training.

The aftermath was a muddled scene of near misses and stark revelations. The patient survived, but the damage done was irreversible. Her eyes, once expressive and lively, were now a vacant testament to Leo's incompetence. She would never blink again, her eyelids rendered useless by his botched attempts at correction.

This incident, though not fatal, marked a turning point in the career of Dr. Leo. It was a glaring spotlight on all that was wrong with his approach—his overconfidence, his disregard for the standards of medical practice, and his manipulative charm that could no longer mask his professional inadequacies.

Word of the incident spread rapidly, as such stories often do, fueled by the whispers of scandal and the shock of the community. Leo's clinic, once a place where hopes were pinned and dreams of beauty conceived, became a cautionary tale about the dangers of unchecked ambition and the peril of placing trust in unverified hands.

The legal repercussions were swift and severe. Complaints were lodged, investigations launched, and Leo's makeshift medical empire began to crumble. The authorities, once indifferent to the whispers of his unorthodox practices, were now diligent in their pursuit of justice. Leo found himself under scrutiny, his every move watched, his clinic raided, and his credentials—or lack thereof—questioned.

In the cold light of day, Leo had to face the consequences of his actions. The law was catching up with him, and the community he had deceived was no longer his audience but his accusers. The woman he had harmed, though silent in her permanent condition, was a loud echo of his failures and the risks he had imposed on others.

As the walls closed in, Leo's options dwindled. The charm that had once opened doors now seemed a flimsy defense against the harsh reality of legal and ethical accountability. He was cornered, a fugitive in his own land, hunted by the consequences of his own hubris.

In this unfolding drama, Leo—once the master of illusions—found himself painfully grounded in reality. The masks were off, the curtains pulled back, and what remained was the stark truth of a man who had flown too close to the sun, his wings of deceit melted by the heat of his own reckless ambition.

This stark realization was a bitter pill to swallow. It forced Leo to reckon with the fact that his life, built on falsehoods and cosmetic enhancements, could not withstand the scrutiny of truth. His career as a doctor was effectively over, his reputation in ruins, and his future uncertain. In a final twist of irony, the man who had tried to sculpt perfection in others was left to ponder the imperfections in his own life, a life now marred by scandal and the shadows of a crime that was not murderous but was morally devastating, nonetheless.

However, in the crash cart, a crucial element for responding to such emergencies, the endotracheal tubes were missing, an inexcusable oversight that exacerbated an already tense situation. The urgency to intubate the patient to ensure her oxygenation turned into a frantic call to 911, a race against time and death. The wait for an ambulance, in a context where every second counts, was prolonged by the deplorable conditions of the route, marked by potholes that not only pose a danger to the physical integrity of vehicles but, in critical situations like this one, can mean the difference between life and death.

In the midst of the mounting tension, a critical exchange took place between Dr. Leo and his nurse: --"How is it possible that there are no endotracheal tubes in the crash cart?" --asked the nurse, her voice tinged with panic and reproach. --"This is not the time for pointless questions. Take care of calling 911 now," --responded Dr. Leo, trying to maintain calm but his voice revealed the tension. --"This wouldn't have happened if we had checked the equipment before starting!" --insisted the nurse anesthetist, as she ran to make the emergency call.

When the authorities finally arrived at Dr. Leo's clinic, following the adverse event that had occurred, they encountered a situation that bordered on chaotic. The affected patient had been receiving oxygen through an Ambu bag for over 90 minutes, a desperate attempt to keep her alive in the absence of an adequate oxygen tank. Curiously, the clinic had a tank of nitrous oxide but not of oxygen, a detail that evidenced a lack of preparation and negligence in the clinic's administration.

The absence of clinic use credentials and the omission of proper sedatives and anesthetics for anesthesia in the emergency kit were indicative of a much larger problem. It was not only a violation of basic medical regulations but pointed to a serious oversight by Dr. Leo and his team. The severity of this situation not only compromised Dr. Leo's medical practice but also highlighted deficiencies in patient care and safety.

Prolonged time without adequate oxygenation has devastating consequences for the human brain. Oxygen deprivation leads to the premature death of brain cells, neurons, affecting various vital functions and, in extreme cases like this, resulting in an irreversible coma due to massive cell death. For the patient, a lady who had been suggested a simple eyelid lift as a solution to her aesthetic concerns, the outcome was tragically irrevocable.

All this unique event at the clinic further enraged the spirit of Julio Leonardo, the architect of all these unnatural disasters.

VIII

The relevant authorities from the health department investigated the events. It took over six months until Dr. Leo was finally charged for not possessing the proper certification for the specialty he practiced, operating a clinic without the necessary permits, and handling medications without the required certifications for their dispensation. Additionally, his clinic was shut down, leaving him waiting for what the examining board and the department of justice would decide about his case.

This ignited the beast that had been dormant inside Julio Leo. Although he submitted to the dictates of the local and federal laws, he did not hide his anger towards them as improper agencies to carry out such acts against a supreme being like him, with the knowledge he had acquired, the many problems he had solved, and the thousands of cosmetic issues that had turned out well. For a simple complication in a patient who had a genetic problem metabolizing anesthetic drugs, he was accused of attempted second-degree murder. The case would not hold up with a good lawyer.

The past six months had been a vortex of despair for Dr. Leo. With his clinic sealed under the weight of the law and his sources of income evaporating like water in the desert, he found himself trapped in a professional and personal limbo. The only thing that seemed to offer him any solace was the illusion of having reconnected with his former girlfriend through social networks, a mirage of a network that he nourished with the false belief that she was somehow back in his life. But this belief was just a game of his own mind; in reality, she had not agreed to such a reunion, at least not with the sincerity or enthusiasm he imagined. For him, Amarilis had become a new toy in the vast digital world, a friendship on the networks that he distorted to satisfy his wounded ego.

Those same social networks, which once served him to build his image and attract clients eager for beautification, now became his refuge, a place where social distances and the barriers of reality faded away. In this parallel universe, he could reinvent himself, at least temporarily, as the prince of his own story, a loyal and desired leader, far from the complications and consequences of his actions in the real world. The networks, in their magnificence, allowed that transformation, erasing with every "like" and comment the image of a man whose career was crumbling under the weight of his own mistakes. But even in this digital realm, the reality of his situation loomed, reminding him that the castle he had built in the air was founded on sand, likely to crumble at the slightest whisper of truth.

During those endless six months, Leo's obsession with Amarilis found no rest. Under the guise of courtesy and unrequited love, he continued to invade her digital life with insinuations and proposals that bordered on fantasy. He spoke of imaginary scenarios where she became his indispensable companion in the professional realm, hinting at a future where they would work side by side in his office, in an endless cycle of day and night.

Amarilis, unaware of the shadows that can harbor human hearts, had no idea of the controversy surrounding the figure of Dr. Leo. The information about the incident that had led to the closure of his clinic and the subsequent legal investigations seemed to have diluted in the sea of daily news, not reaching the prominence such events would have had if the involved doctor came from foreign lands. On the island, issues involving local medical professionals, especially those wrapped in the glamour of cosmetic surgery, often remained in the background, overshadowed by a mix of community protectionism and the constant distraction of other scandals. If the incident had occurred abroad, newspapers would have filled their pages with stories proclaiming the superiority of local aestheticians, ensuring that such misfortunes do not happen to them.

Thus, while Amarilis navigated her life, oblivious to the storms battering Leo's world, he clung to the digital illusion he had created one in which he could, eventually, make Amarilis an integral part of his rebuilt life. But this fantasy, built on the sands of desperation and desire, overlooked the essential truth that human connections cannot be forged or sustained on deceit and manipulation. Unknowingly, Leo was weaving his own web of loneliness, one in which the figure of Amarilis shone like an unreachable beacon, beyond the fog of his own schemes.

The decisive day had arrived, a critical moment in which Dr. Leo felt the urgent need to confront the emotional whirlwind that had been brewing within him. The idea of asking Amarilis out was not merely a whim; it was an act laden with significance, a desperate attempt to insert her into the chaos now defining his existence, marked by the scandal of the affected patient. It was a personal crossroads, a turning point: either Amarilis became his accomplice, his salvation amidst the disaster, or she would be relegated to oblivion, excluded from his life altogether. He would possess her, or she would belong to no one.

However, Amarilis, with an intuition sharpened by circumstances, once again regarded Leo's persistent pleas with suspicion. His offer, disguised as a professional opportunity, was nothing more than another attempt to entrap her in his turbulent world. Once again, she chose to decline the invitation, a decision that ignited flames of rage in Leo to unprecedented levels.

How dare she, he thought, to scorn his advances? Who did this woman think she was, who, even adorned with the physical enhancements he so desired, remained in his mind a lesser figure, a shadow in the grand scheme of his life? In his distorted perception, Amarilis's refusal became an act of aggression towards him, an unacceptable disdain that he could not, and would not, tolerate. No one had dared to challenge him in such a way, let alone someone he considered insignificant.

This rejection not only ignited the beast of fury within him but also plunged him into a sea of resentment and grievance. To Leo, facing Amarilis's refusal was to confront a direct attack on his ego, an affront that triggered in him an irrational desire for revenge and domination. In his mind, Amarilis had committed the worst of crimes: that of rejecting him, of denying him the adoration and submission he believed he deserved by right. And so, in his dark reasoning, he began to devise a plan, driven not by love, but by the impulse to subdue and control whoever dared to defy him.

Dr. Leo, in his growing obsession, did not relent in his analog siege on Amarilis. With an almost religious constancy, he praised every comment, every photo, even celebrating her most trivial achievements with a fervor bordering on the implausible. This adulation was nothing more than a stratagem, a carefully constructed mirage of his own image, designed to dazzle Amarilis and reconquer her, to possess her again as in those days that still resonated with the memory of their first encounter when he violated her virginity.

In this electronic dance of seduction, both presented profiles transformed by their respective cosmetic surgeries. Dr. Leo's features had been altered to such an extent that they were almost unrecognizable, a permanent mask hiding the original face Amarilis had known. Meanwhile, the modifications to Amarilis's body were so striking that they unleashed in Julio Leo a mixture of admiration, sexual passion, and vehement desire, a whirlwind of emotions that clouded his judgment.

Every day, Leo wove his net tighter, trying to trap Amarilis in an illusion of mutual affection and admiration. He used every digital tool at his disposal, from direct messages full of praise to public comments painting a picture of himself as the perfect admirer, the only one capable of truly appreciating the changes Amarilis had chosen for herself.

However, behind this facade of devotion and charm lurked a game of power and control, a sinister plot of siege masked in intrigue and gallantry. Leo was determined not to leave a stone unturned in his effort to envelop Amarilis in his world once more, ready to use his influence and omnipresent presence on social media to ensure that, if he couldn't have her by conventional means, he would have her by persistence, manipulation, and even force if necessary. His once lucid and rational mind was now consumed by the vision of possessing Amarilis, no matter the cost, sliding ever deeper into the abysses of obsession.

In a desperate and risky act, Dr. Leo decided to send Amarilis an invitation to visit his clinic, despite it having been closed down by local authorities following the incident that sparked a scandal. His medical license had been temporarily suspended while the Department of Justice investigated the case, a devastating blow to his practice and reputation.

Nevertheless, Leo, driven by a mix of challenge and an irrational desire to impress Amarilis, retained the key to the clinic. He saw in this key not only physical access to the building but also an opportunity to deploy a final play of charm and persuasion. He planned to show Amarilis the space, perhaps in an attempt to evoke nostalgia for better days or to demonstrate some semblance of normalcy and control over his professional life, despite the storm looming over him.

In an ominous detail, the sedative medications he usually used in his procedures had not yet been confiscated. This fact added a layer of potential danger to the visit, as these medications, in the wrong hands or used without proper care, could pose a significant risk.

This invitation, therefore, was not simply a gesture of transparency or an attempt to resume normal operations; it was an act charged with hidden intentions and desperation. Leo was playing on dangerous ground, manipulating circumstances in his favor, hoping that Amarilis's presence in the closed clinic, surrounded by echoes of its former glory and the not-so-distant dangers, might somehow reignite their lost connection and convince her of his worth and status, despite the clear signs of his downfall.

IX

Finally, Amarilis yielded to Dr. Leo's persistent requests. After much insistence, they agreed on a specific date and time for her to visit the facilities of the closed aesthetic clinic. Amarilis, guided more by cautious fear than admiration, wanted to see for herself if she could truly consider joining Leo's practice, even though this place was currently shrouded in shadows of doubt and scandal.

With the agreed-upon appointment, what at first glance seemed like a simple professional meeting unwittingly turned into preparation for a final siege. Amarilis, unknowingly, had marked on her calendar the date of a meeting that could have dire consequences. She was about to enter the siege of an individual who, beyond his charming and persuasive manners, hid a dark and disturbing past.

Dr. Leo, who had been expelled from his residency in surgery for inappropriate behavior, had built a false identity as a cosmetic surgeon. His career culminated tragically in a serious incident, where a young patient suffered irreversible brain damage due to lack of oxygen during a procedure, a result of mishandled sedation and cardiopulmonary arrest. This event had devastated the patient's life, condemning her to a perpetual vegetative state.

This meeting, arranged under the pretext of a job opportunity, was charged with an ominous air. Amarilis, though not fully aware of the gravity of the situation, was approaching a critical moment that would define much more than her professional future. She was entering, perhaps, the most dangerous phase of her relationship with Dr. Leo, a man whose ability to inflict harm had been demonstrated, and whose intentions could be anything but benign.

Four years ago, Julio Leo had gifted his mother a black Ford Bronco, a Mother's Day gift marking a moment of prosperity and apparent generosity in his life. However, the fortune he had amassed through his clinic had been drastically diminished, leading him to surrender his BMW M3 convertible to the bank due to an inability to keep up with the payments. This contrast between past ostentation and current financial reality reflected Leo's downfall, not only personally but also professionally.

On the agreed-upon day for the meeting with Amarilis, Leo arrived at the closed clinic an hour earlier than scheduled. With a mix of anticipation and dark meticulousness, he prepared what he deemed necessary for the appointment. It was not a typical preparation for a job interview; instead of documents or presentations, Leo arranged a tray of sterile instruments including a Bard-Parker number twelve scalpel and various surgical forceps, items that boded ill.

Alongside these instruments, he placed a potent barbiturate in aerosol form and injectable Ketamine, a strong hypnotic. These preparations were not those of someone planning to simply discuss a job offer, but rather those of someone preparing for a much more sinister and controlling encounter.

This scene prepared by Leo revealed a plan with nefarious intentions, disclosing the depth of his desperation and possibly his desire to fully control the situation, extending to dominating Amarilis's will and decisions. The early arrival and meticulous preparations indicated a desire to ensure that nothing stood in his way, planning every detail with a precision that was both impressive and alarming. The transformation of a space that was once dedicated to healing into the stage for a macabre plan symbolized the total corruption of Leo's character and professional ethics.

Amarilis arrived punctually for the appointment, her heart pounding as she gazed from outside at the impressive facilities now before her. With trembling hands, she rang the doorbell of the main entrance and waited, submerged in a mix of anticipation and buried fear. Dr. Leo, aware of the doorbell sound, deliberately let a few seconds pass, cultivating an air of calculated calmness before opening the door. There he was, clad in his medical authority, the white coat outlining his name and specialty in embroidered letters contrasting with the pure white.

--"Good afternoon, I presume you are Nurse Amarilis?" Dr. Leo asked, although he knew the answer perfectly well.

Amarilis, with a hint of panic in her eyes and the unsettling sensation of reliving an episode from her past, said with a trembling voice:

--"Miss Amarilis Cintron, at your service," --and after a pause, she added with a thread of voice-- "I don't know, but it seems to me that I know you from somewhere before, doctor."

Leo, with a quick response intended to dispel suspicions, replied:

--"Perhaps from when I was training in the United States."

--"Excuse me, but maybe it's my mistake, although I trained locally at the medical sciences facility," --uncertainty began to erode Amarilis's confidence, while a foreboding feeling enveloped her.

--"No matter, Dr. Leo at your service. Come this way to see the aesthetic clinic," --the doctor commented, uneasy at the possibility of being recognized.

As Amarilis transitioned from the luxurious waiting area to the secretary's cubicle, adorned with an impressive oil painting of a blue Morpho butterfly, she tried with all her might to remember where she had seen that doctor before, whose gaze and tone of voice evoked memories she wished had been erased forever.

Leo guided Amarilis through the labyrinth of cubicles in his office, each with its own secrets and echoes of past procedures. They entered a particularly gloomy room, a minor procedure room that housed a macabre collection of medical devices: an anesthesia machine, devices for measuring oxygen in the blood, and capnography monitors. Here, the air still seemed to resonate with the echo of a nefarious incident; a previous patient had suffered respiratory arrest due to a miscalculated dose of regional anesthesia. Now, she lay inert, a shadow of her former self in a healthcare facility, a mute testimony to the doctor's incompetence that had led to the closure of his practice.

Beyond this room, two additional cubicles stretched out: one was a modest corner equipped for food preparation and consumption, presenting a facade of normalcy amidst the abnormality of the place. The other, more intimate, housed a simple bed intended for rest or, perhaps, less innocent purposes. These spaces, hidden behind the clinical facade of the office, were Leo's personal domains, corners where daily routine mingled with the potential for darker and lonelier acts.

But it was upon entering Dr. Leo's main cubicle, sitting in the chair intended for patients, that a silent scream of terror unleashed within her. Suddenly, the blood in her veins turned to ice. Before her hung a reproduction of the diploma that Julio had falsified, proclaiming himself a general surgeon from a prestigious program when Amarilis knew he had been expelled.

The most terrifying blow to Amarilis's fragility came when she clearly read the name 'Julio Leonardo Salazar' on the documentation. A chill of recognition ran through her. She remained motionless, her gaze fixed on the diploma, as the doctor left the room. Her mind flooded with tortuous memories, that tumultuous past with this man who now returned to her present.

The self-administered surgery by Leo had altered his physiognomy with the skill of a sculptor obsessed with his own image. The ptosis of his eyelids had been corrected; his eyelids now suggested no hint of weakness or tiredness. His chin, previously concealed by lack of definition, now rose with determined prominence. The nose, once perhaps too distinctive, had been softened in its contours, and the lips, in an attempt to follow modern beauty standards, appeared slightly fuller, hinting at a rejuvenated youth. All hidden under a thick dark beard.

However, in the fervor to renew his face, Leo hadn't accounted for Amarilis's unyielding memory. The eyes, although now surrounded by rejuvenated tissue, remained the same: two dark wells hiding stories Amarilis would have preferred to forget. Her voice, that particular cadence that couldn't be disguised even with the best of artifices, betrayed any attempt by Leo to mask his past. It was this immutability in her gaze and tone that undoubtedly betrayed him to Amarilis, connecting the present with memories she believed buried.

Sweating profusely under her dress, soaked with unfathomable fear, she went over every fragment of those dark chapters of her life, reliving the brutal moment when Julio had violated her against her will, the pain he had inflicted, the blood he had shed.

As soon as Dr. Leo perceived the emerging pallor on Amarilis's face and saw her eyes flash with recognition of danger, he knew it was time to act. With a skill that belied his apparent calm demeanor, he soaked a surgical towel with a barbiturate in aerosol form. He stealthily brought it closer to Amarilis's cheeks, with a gentleness bordering on perversity, hoping that, in her desperate attempt to free herself, she would voraciously inhale the anesthetic dispersed in the air.

Amarilis, struggling for every breath and yearning to escape, inadvertently breathed more deeply, accelerating the absorption of the hypnotic dissolving with each inhalation. Darkness began to close in on her like a curtain, as her eyelids grew heavy under the influence of the sedative. And so, in a blink that seemed to stretch eternally, Amarilis was plunged into an abyssal sleep, a lethargy from which her terrified and lonely consciousness feared she might never wake up.

Barely had Amarilis been plunged into the twilight of unconsciousness when Dr. Leo, with disturbing serenity and precise movements, extracted the calculated amount of ketamine from a vial. His needle pierced the skin of Amarilis's left deltoid muscle with surgical precision, injecting the twenty-five milligrams of the potent substance. Almost instantly, the drug spread through her system, dragging Amarilis into a hypnotic trance, an abyss of drowsiness from which she could neither, nor knew how to, escape.

In this dissociative state, where reality intertwines with hallucinations, Nurse Amarilis was adrift, floating in a darkness where the boundaries of her being seemed to fade away. She was a puppet in the hands of Dr. Leo, whose countenance hid the most sinister intentions behind the mask of a caregiver. With his helpless victim before him, Leo began to plot his next step, guided by a scheming mind that planned to exploit that state of vulnerability to the fullest. Amarilis, submerged in the sopor induced by ketamine, was oblivious to the dark designs surrounding her, lost in a nightmare from which she was not certain she could awaken.

Consumed by an obsessive and perverse desire, Leo longed to seize Amarilis, to subject her to his will and turn her into an object of his possession. His mind, quick and disturbed, considered the possibility of moving her to the quiet room at the back of the clinic, the one that housed a modest cot intended for rest. However, the idea was discarded as soon as it arose, aware that any future investigation could reveal the nefarious acts committed within those four walls.

Instead, Leo, with a pragmatism as cold as his intention, opted to transport Amarilis in the back of his black Ford Bronco. Carefully, he placed her in the vehicle, ensuring she was not visible from the outside. With an ominous hum, the engine roared to life and glided through the streets, moving away from the clinic, and taking with it the nurse, now a victim of his dark purposes.

The destination was a dubious reputation motel in Caguas, a place where he could carry out his malevolent intentions away from prying eyes, a site where loneliness and anonymity provided the necessary veil to hide his actions. Amarilis's transition from the security of her everyday life to the confinement of that vehicle, at the hands of a man whose mind harbored only shadows, was a testimony to the terrifying turn her reality had taken.

Upon arriving at the dubious reputation motel, Leo paid for the room in an environment where discretion was the norm and observation, a forgotten art. With calculated methods, he transported Amarilis's still insensible body to the round bed dominating the room. In an attempt to create a less sordid atmosphere, he played romantic music by Luis Miguel and poured himself a shot of pure tequila, believing in the old myth that it could revive dormant passions.

In addition to the rotating round bed, adorned with several cushions showing clear signs of frequent use, the room was equipped with a huge mirror, also round, placed on the ceiling. This mirror, strategically positioned, allowed the occupants of the bed to observe in detail the actions that took place beneath it, capturing the movements of the lovers in a unique and voyeuristic perspective.

Completing the facilities of the temporary apartment was a modest ablution bathroom, whose dimensions and equipment were just sufficient for the basic needs of those who rented the room for a few hours. This small sanitary space, though functional, contrasted with the ostentation and decadence suggested by the rotating bed and ceiling mirror, offering a somber reminder of the transient and merely superficial nature of the place.

With a mixture of desire and caution, Leo began to undress Amarilis slowly. There was no rush in his movements, not for fear that she would awaken — the sedatives took care of that — but out of care not to damage her delicate clothing or, more critically, not to deteriorate her meticulously remodeled body. As he stripped Amarilis of her clothes, his eyes couldn't help but linger on her reconstructed breasts, testaments to a carefully chosen aesthetic.

Subdued by the sight of her breasts, Leo began to caress them gently, salivating and sucking each nipple with growing fervor. Although immersed in a deep lethargy due to the sedatives, Amarilis's body instinctively reacted to the contact; small convulsions of pleasure that she herself could neither recognize nor, much less, consent to in her state of unconsciousness. These involuntary gestures of Amarilis were ignored by Leo, whose actions were guided solely by his darkest and most depraved impulses, in a scenario where morality had been displaced by coercion and control.

He carefully slid Amarilis's panties off, exposing the delicate intimacy of her body. With an invasive gesture, he moistened with his lips the erogenous zone lying before him, evoking the image of a butterfly with its wings outstretched. He meticulously explored with his tongue, eliciting an involuntary reaction that released glandular secretions in response to the incessant stimulation.

He continued his predatory act, penetrating repeatedly, each thrust seeking his own climax in a frenetic succession of orgasms. Under the heavy curtain of the sedatives, Amarilis, in an altered state and unaware of her will, seemed to physically respond to the manipulations to which she was subjected, a grotesque distortion of pleasure amidst the violation.

This deeply macabre and disturbing scene unfolded while Amarilis's consciousness remained eclipsed by the chemistry of the sedatives, her body reacting reflexively to stimuli that her mind was not in a position to process or consent to.

Julio, in an act of continued brutality, turned Amarilis's body to access her from another position. Not content with violating her vaginally, he also subjected her to an anal assault, leaving a trail of his DNA in the form of semen along her body, the anal area, and the motel bed sheets. These acts not only marked his physical dominance but also inadvertently sowed crucial evidence for future investigations.

After violating her from behind, with calculated cruelty, Julio inserted his still erect penis into Amarilis's mouth. In a final act of contempt, he ejaculated, depositing his semen in her mouth. This vile act pretended to be a grotesque gesture of feeding her with his genetic essence, a way to mark his total control over her even in the most intimate and personal aspects.

These acts of rape not only left physical and emotional scars on Amarilis but also scattered evidence of Julio's crime throughout the scene of the assault. It would be through these semen samples, ruthlessly deposited by

Julio, that the final act would eventually be connected to its perpetrator, revealing his identity as the perpetrator of this horrendous crime.

Julio took a brief respite, resting on the round bed of the motel for thirty minutes, recovering before continuing with his cruel sexual assault. However, he had not anticipated that the effects of the sedatives would begin to diminish in Amarilis's system, who gradually began to regain consciousness amidst this horrifying situation.

When Julio began his assault again, this time directly facing Amarilis, her eyes slowly began to open, returning to the cruel reality of her pain and the recognition of the attack she was enduring. As he penetrated her, Amarilis began to perceive the source of the intense pain; a cruel and clear lucidity appeared in her gaze, a sign that she was beginning to understand the magnitude of the atrocious violation to which she was being subjected.

This partial awakening, in the midst of the violent act, added a layer of psychological terror to the already unbearable physical torment. Amarilis, now partially conscious, found herself trapped in a reality where each movement of Julio became a torture amplified by the growing understanding of her vulnerable and desperate situation.

In a desperate attempt at defense, Amarilis managed to push Julio, causing him to lose his balance and fall to the ground. However, he quickly recovered from the stumble. With agile and calculated movements, Julio headed towards his briefcase of instruments that he always carried with him, extracting from it a Bard-Parker brand number 12 scalpel. Amarilis, still weak, remained under the influence of medication.

With a cold and methodical precision, reflecting his surgical training, Julio made a transverse and meticulous incision in the anterior and lower part of Amarilis's neck as she lunged at him again in her weakness. The incision, deep and precise, brutally opened her respiratory tract, exposing the vulnerability of her existence in that unheard-of act of violence. This act not only sought to physically subdue Amarilis but also symbolized an extreme and disturbing control, marking a point of no return in Julio's spiral of ruthless actions.

After the brutal cut in the trachea, Amarilis began to experience the devastating effects of the inflicted wound. As blood flowed copiously, further obstructing her already compromised respiratory system, oxygen ceased to reach her brain efficiently. Cerebral hypoxia, a state of oxygen deficit in the brain, began to take control of her body, initiating a silent but lethal process.

In the following minutes, Amarilis fought for every breath in a desperate and futile effort to survive. Both hands clung to her neck, the origin of her asphyxiation. Each inhalation was a painful challenge, and each exhalation a reminder of her imminent end. The oxygen necessary to maintain her basic brain functions was drastically reduced, causing acute mental confusion, blurred vision, and an intensifying feeling of dizziness with each passing second.

Gradually, reality faded for Amarilis as she fell into a state of semi-consciousness; her world reduced to fragments of disjointed and distorted perceptions. Her ability to think clearly or respond to the environment dissipated as quickly as the oxygen in her blood. Eventually, the effects of hypoxia solidified, and Amarilis found herself trapped in an internal battle for life, a battle that tilted increasingly towards a fatal outcome.

Julio Leo had consummated the most heinous act; he had murdered his victim after ruthlessly abusing her. The life of an innocent woman had been cruelly cut short by his hands. After committing the act, a sense of panic flooded Julio as he realized the magnitude of his crime. He looked around, horrified by the scene of brutality he had created.

In a state of frantic nervousness, he quickly gathered his belongings. Every movement was imbued with the urgency to flee and the fear of being discovered. With compulsive meticulousness, he searched the place for any evidence that could incriminate him in the premeditated and monstrous murder of Amarilis. Making sure not to leave traces of his presence or his vile act, Julio moved with a mixture of speed and caution.

Finally convinced that he had erased all possible clues, Julio hastily left the crime scene. His mind was in turmoil, agitated by the fear of the consequences of his actions and the temporary relief of having eliminated the evidence of his crime. He hurried away as fast as he could, disappearing into the shadow of the night, carrying with him the weight of his guilt and the ghost of the life he had taken.

The lifeless body of Amarilis lay abandoned in the center of the motel's round bed, her neck marked by a deep cut in the trachea, a silent testimony to the violence suffered. This was how she was found when the motel staff, often indifferent and neglectful, decided to check the room because the time paid for by the guest had expired and they had not emerged from the room.

The scene they encountered was gruesome: amidst the artificial opulence of the rotating bed and the worn cushions, Amarilis's figure seemed particularly tragic and desolate. This routine check soon turned into a case for the authorities: the administrators, surpassing their usual apathy, called the local police.

With the arrival of the officers, Amarilis's tragic fate began to be officially documented. The area was cordoned off, and what began as a standard procedure for checking on a late guest turned into a criminal investigation. The beautiful Amarilis, now reduced to a victim of a ruthless act, lay at the center of a whirlwind of police activity.

There, in that anonymous and sordid place, Amarilis remained, forever captured by death at the hands of a psychopath who had disappeared as abruptly as he had entered her life, leaving behind a trail of horror and consternation.

Leo, in a calculated attempt to unlink himself from any physical evidence that could connect him to the crime, chose to get rid of the Ford Bronco. He knew that the vehicle, used during the atrocious act, could become a key piece in the investigation if it was associated with him. To ensure that the car disappeared without a trace, he sold it to a known dealer of used cars with a dubious reputation, nicknamed "Jaime's Junker".

Jaime, the dealer in question, had a fairly lucrative business eliminating cars that might be implicated in criminal activities. For a sum of two thousand dollars, he took care of making any suspicious vehicle "evaporate", ensuring that there was no tangible evidence that could link those cars to their previous owners in illicit contexts.

This elimination of evidence was a critical part of his service, facilitating individuals like Leo to distance themselves from their crimes with a lower probability of being discovered.

In Leo's case, besides getting rid of the vehicle, there were no direct evidences connecting him to the victim, except for some sporadic interactions on social media that, without additional context, were inconclusive. This lack of clear and direct connections to the deceased Amarilis, combined with the disappearance of the Ford Bronco, was part of his strategy to remain as a ghost in the investigation, a barely perceptible specter on the periphery of the authorities.

X

Alfredo Montesino, the astute private investigator hired by Amarilis's grieving family to uncover the circumstances of her tragic murder, was immersed in his work. His desk was cluttered with documents and evidence meticulously gathered during the investigation. After conducting a series of deep and revealing interviews with Amarilis's closest relatives in her hometown of Moca, Alfredo had begun to piece together important clues.

Reflecting intensely on the details of the crime from the comfort of his terrace, Alfredo Montesino, the private investigator in charge of Amarilis's case, sat with crossed legs on his desk, savoring the taste of a Heineken beer while the wind toyed with the bottle cap, creating a soft whisper that accompanied his thoughts.

As he digested the gathered information and planned his next moves, Alfredo dreamed of solving the case. He imagined collecting the reward agreed upon for his hard work and, perhaps this time, allowing himself a well-deserved break on the exotic island of Moorea in the Polynesian. This place, famous for being one of the refuges of the celebrated Paul Gauguin, who settled there after leaving behind the figure of an aging and decadent Van Gogh, seemed like the perfect destination to escape the routine and chaos of his current work.

The idea of walking the same paths that Gauguin explored and where he painted his iconic and voluptuous figures provided Alfredo with a sense of connection to art and history, a refreshing contrast to the dark and often dangerous world of criminal investigation. In that moment of introspection, Montesino saw himself not only as a detective seeking justice but also as a traveler in search of inspiration and peace, far from the grim details of his daily work.

This diligent agent managed to secure interviews with two key figures who could shed light on the case: Angel

Marcel, who had recently forged a friendship with the victim and was emerging as a crucial witness due to his temporal proximity to the events; and the enigmatic Doctor Leo, a personality hiding behind a facade of medical respectability. Both characters were of paramount interest in the investigation, and Alfredo meticulously prepared for these encounters, aware that any detail they could offer would be vital to unraveling the mystery surrounding Amarilis's death.

With a systematic approach and an analytical mind, Montesino continuously reviewed the notes and evidence gathered, searching for inconsistencies or clues that would allow him to construct a coherent narrative of the events. He was determined to get to the truth, not only to bring justice to Amarilis's family but also to ensure that a dangerous murderer was captured and could not harm anyone else.

During his meeting with Angel Marcel, Alfredo Montesino quickly perceived the depth of affection this man had developed for Amarilis. Evidence of an unrequited and recently interrupted love was palpable; Angel had fallen into a noticeable depression after the brutal murder of the young woman. Alfredo examined the various pieces of evidence: romantic interactions on social media, the heartfelt comments from Amarilis's parents, and, above all, the emotional initial interview with Angel, where tears had flowed freely as he recounted feeling unfairly treated as a suspect in the homicide of the woman he admired and wished to court.

This accumulation of emotions and evidence made it clear to Alfredo that Angel was deeply impacted by the tragedy. He had openly wept during the interview, expressing his pain and frustration at being involved in the investigation as a possible suspect when he was actually dealing with the loss of someone he had begun to genuinely care for. The investigator noticed that every memory of Amarilis invoked in Angel a storm of sadness and desolation, revealing a genuinely affected and broken heart by the violence that had ripped Amarilis from this world.

Alfredo Montesino had come to the definitive conclusion that Angel Marcel, despite his emotional complications and his history of relationships with both men and women, did not possess the physical capability or the coldness necessary to handle a scalpel with the intention of lethally harming someone. The idea of Angel inflicting a fatal cut to someone's neck was inconceivable; he simply did not have the constitution or the temperament to commit such a brutal act. Angel, in Alfredo's opinion, was more of a schemer who used his charm to manipulate others, a gigolo who would not risk getting his hands dirty in an act of direct violence.

In contrast, Doctor Leo, the other main suspect in the case, exhibited a completely different profile. His medical background and access to surgical instruments made him a much more likely candidate to have performed such a meticulous and fatal cut as the one Amarilis had suffered.

Additionally, his enigmatic personality and his possible ability to conceal a darker nature behind a facade of professionalism endowed him with the attributes necessary to be considered a true suspect in this heinous crime.

Determined to pursue this more promising line of investigation, Alfredo chose to concentrate his efforts on unraveling the mysteries surrounding Dr. Leo. He was determined to explore every aspect of his professional and personal life, convinced that there he would find the keys to solving Amarilis's murder. The investigation would intensify with a renewed focus, aiming to unmask any hint of guilt that might be hidden in the apparently respectable existence of the doctor.

During his meticulous interview with Dr. Leo, Alfredo Montesino had posed a series of carefully crafted questions to assess the doctor's reaction and look for inconsistencies in his account. Although some of Leo's answers had raised suspicions in Alfredo, indicating that he might be facing the murderer, he still lacked concrete evidence to proceed with a formal accusation.

The investigator knew he needed a more solid link to legally implicate Dr. Leo in Amarilis's murder. The black Ford Bronco, a key element in Amarilis's disappearance, was not listed in the doctor's vehicle records, making it difficult to establish a direct connection. Furthermore, the other vehicle Leo owned had already been handed over to the authorities for inspection, with no significant findings that could be used against him.

The situation regarding Dr. Leo's professional practice was also complex. His clinic had been closed, a detail that added a shadow of doubt over his professional activities. Even more incriminating, Leo's medical certification to practice was currently suspended by the country's medical examining board, raising questions about his conduct and professional ethics.

Alfredo found himself at a critical point in the investigation. Despite the suspicions and clues pointing towards Dr. Leo as a potential culprit, the lack of concrete physical evidence and the doctor's ability to maintain a facade of legality complicated any attempts to formally accuse him. The investigator knew he needed to keep searching, delving deeper into Leo's life and background to find the missing piece that could ultimately connect him to Amarilis's brutal murder.

In his exhaustive search for clues, Alfredo Montesino stumbled upon a crucial detail that further complicated the case: the analysis of the genetic material found at the crime scene. The collected semen, a potentially decisive piece of evidence, did not match any of the known suspects' genetic profiles to date, including Dr. Leo's.

The absence of the doctor's DNA in previous prisoners' genetic records was not unusual given his lack of criminal history, but it added a layer of difficulty to the investigation. This meant that if Dr. Leo was indeed the culprit, he had managed to avoid leaving conclusive traces of his DNA in previous legal situations, not only indicating his possible care to avoid being caught but also posing a significant challenge to directly linking him to the crime through genetic evidence.

Alfredo faced the possibility that the killer might have been extremely cautious, or worse, that there might have been more than one person involved in Amarilis's murder and that the true culprit might still not be on the police's radar. The investigation, therefore, required even greater review and expansion, exploring not only the known possible connections but also those that might have remained hidden or unexpected.

This situation forced Alfredo to consider new strategies and possibly to collaborate more closely with forensic authorities to track any other type of evidence that might be available, hoping to find some clue that could finally lead to identifying the true perpetrator of the crime.

Seated across from Leo, Alfredo Montesino posed a crucial question, seeking clarity on a matter he considered essential to understanding the doctor's profile:

--"So, Doctor, can you explain to me why you left the surgical residency, please?" --he asked in a tone that denoted the seriousness of the investigation.

--"Well, it so happened that a professor of pediatric surgery during that clinical rotation took issue with me because he alleged that I wasn't doing my job well. His personal low ratings encouraged the department group to have me removed from my position," --Leo responded, deliberately omitting any mention of how he used to mark the internal cavities of patients with his initials or how operating room staff had filed formal complaints accusing him of mutilation with the use of the laparoscope. What Leo was unaware of was that Montesino had already visited the surgery department of the medical sciences campus before the interview and had obtained all that compromising information. Leo wasn't lying per se; he was simply twisting the truth.

Continuing his direct questioning, Alfredo posed another incisive question:

--"Is it true or not true, Doctor, that you used a branding iron-type cautery on surgical patients, including pediatric ones?" --inquired Montesino.

--"That's not true!" --Leo responded vehemently. --"It may be that with the misplaced laparoscopic cautery control someone from the staff accidentally stepped on the floor control and we cauterized something additional that we didn't anticipate, but not as I was accused, agent," --Leo defended himself, trying to downplay his responsibility for the acts he was accused of.

Alfredo continued with the basic questions to better understand the doctor's background:

--"Did you have a black Ford Bronco vehicle, Doctor?" --

--"I bought one for my mom a long time ago, but it was stolen from the old lady's house, and she didn't report it as she should have," --Leo explained, trying to disassociate himself from any connection with the vehicle in question.

--"Doctor, where did you study medicine?" --

--"At the country's medical school," --Leo said.

--"Did you excel in any branch of medicine?" --

--"In my third year of medicine, I, along with six other classmates, became a permanent member of the medical honor society, Alpha Omega Alpha," --Leo shared, not without a certain pride.

--"Congratulations, Doctor," --granted Montesino, maintaining professional courtesy.

--"Thank you," --Leo responded, accepting the recognition with a mix of satisfaction and caution.

Alfredo Montesino leaned forward, fixing his gaze on Dr. Leo, and repeated his question with a tone demanding clarity:

--"I'll ask again, Doctor, why was your clinic closed a few months ago?" --

Dr. Leo, with measured expression, responded in detail:

--"It so happened that a patient with a genetic disorder we were unaware of experienced a reduction in sedative elimination, going into respiratory arrest and requiring cardiopulmonary resuscitation for an extended period of over an hour. She had signed a consent form where she understood that there is a very low percentage of cases in which patients with genetic defects in drug elimination from the body can experience this described complication." --

Then, with a tone that conveyed both hope and frustration, he added: --"As soon as we are cleared of any criminal wrongdoing, work can resume at the clinic, agent"—

Dr. Leo's response was laden with legal and medical implications, reflecting the complexity of the procedures at his clinic that, according to him, had been temporarily suspended due to an unfortunate yet apparently anticipated event in medical consents.

Alfredo Montesino found himself in a complicated position. Despite his suspicions and the unsettling questions, he had posed during the interview, he had not managed to obtain concrete evidence directly implicating Dr. Leo in the crime. Without solid evidence justifying an arrest or further legal actions, Alfredo was forced to allow the doctor to leave, albeit with a firm and cautious recommendation: --"I ask that you do not leave the country until this crime is clarified, and you are completely exonerated of any suspicion,"-- he indicated, hoping to secure some degree of control over the situation.

Aware that he needed to delve deeper into Dr. Leo's past and connections, Alfredo decided to head to the medical school where Leo had completed his training. His intention was to speak directly with the professors who had been in charge of the doctor's medical education. He thought that by exploring Leo's academic and professional environment, he might discover irregularities or testimonies that had not come to light during preliminary investigations.

Upon arriving at the institution, he began arranging meetings with the teaching staff who knew Dr. Leo closely, seeking to better understand his character, skills, and above all, any past behavior that might be related to the events now linking him to a homicide. Alfredo hoped that these conversations would provide him with the missing information he needed to build a stronger case or, at the very least, to understand the nature of the enigmatic doctor more clearly.

Alfredo Montesino conducted interviews with several of the former professors at the medical school where Dr. Leo had been trained. One of these professors, a prominent pediatric surgeon, was particularly critical of Leo. He expressed dissatisfaction with the student's egocentric character, highlighting that, despite his honors grades, his personality left much to be desired. -- "He was not suitable for promotion,"-- commented the surgeon, referring to a decision he had made to oppose Leo's advancement after a concerning incident with a patient. --"I distinctly remember the case that made me question his professional ethics. A 12-year-old girl was admitted urgently with a diagnosis of twisted ovary. Leo, who was on duty that night, decided not to intervene immediately. His justification was that the necessary procedure was simply to distort the ovary, something that, according to him, could wait until the morning, regardless of the tissue's condition,"-- explained the surgeon with evident frustration.

The professor continued, --"That careless attitude towards a real medical emergency, where every minute counts, was alarming. I couldn't allow someone with such little respect for medical urgency to advance without facing serious repercussions."--

Despite these severe criticisms of his character, other professors at the medical school, while acknowledging his academic ability, also reluctantly admitted that Leo was brilliant academically. --"It's true that he was an honors student, and his grades proved it,"-- they added, contrasting the critique of his ethics with acknowledgments of his academic performance.

Alfredo Montesino received a crucial clue from one of Leo's classmates, who was also a member of the exclusive group of seven high-achieving students named to the Alpha Omega Alpha honor society and was now faculty at the medical school. This information emerged as a flash of clarity amidst what seemed like an unfathomable mystery. Leo's colleague, in a casual tone, revealed something that could be the key to better resolving the situation: --"It's interesting, agent, but Leo complained when we were named to the Alpha Omega Alpha honor society,"-- the doctor mentioned almost inadvertently.

Intrigued, Alfredo delved further into the comment: --"Why do you say that doctor?"--

The physician continued with an explanation that added a completely new dimension to the case: --"It's because the seven of us were asked for a semen sample in the third year of medical school to store it, due to the high academic index and intelligence quotient we had,"-- he explained.

Then, he added details about the purpose of that sample collection: --"It was used to inseminate a patient whose partner had azoospermia, meaning the man did not produce sperm and could not fertilize his partner,"-- and he continued, further clarifying: --"It's a sperm bank of people with a high intelligence quotient, cataloged so that whoever uses it knows more or less the genetic characteristics of the donor."--

This revelation about the sperm bank practice and Leo's resistance to participating in it opened up new lines of investigation that Alfredo could explore, perhaps bringing him one step closer to the truth behind the mysterious case.

The revelation from Leo's colleague turned out to be a piece of immensely relevant information for Alfredo Montesino, illuminating a potentially fruitful path in his investigation. This new nugget of information sparked a strategic idea in the investigator's mind: if he could access Leo's stored genetic material in the sperm bank, he could compare it with the samples collected from the victim at the crime scene. This genetic connection could provide the missing link he had been searching for to strengthen his case against Leo.

He contemplated how Leo's semen, preserved due to his high academic and cognitive value, if matching that found on Amarilis, would not only unequivocally link Leo to the murder scene but could also be the definitive evidence he needed to establish his guilt beyond any reasonable doubt.

With this new lead in hand, Montesino planned his next move: obtaining a court order to access that genetic material. He knew the process could be complicated and would require detailed argumentation before the courts to justify the invasion of privacy and medical confidentiality, but he was determined to pursue this route. The possibility of closing the case with conclusive evidence drove him to move quickly and precisely.

The semen sample of Julio Leo Salazar, meticulously preserved in the medical school's sperm bank, lay frozen, kept at an optimal temperature for conservation. The task facing Alfredo Montesino was significant: he needed to obtain that sample, carefully thaw it, and prepare it for a comprehensive comparative analysis with the genetic material found at the scene of Amarilis's tragic murder.

This process was fraught with emotional tension. On one hand, the possibility of finally connecting Julio to the crime through irrefutable evidence gave Montesino renewed hope for justice for Amarilis. On the other hand, the invasive and technical nature of the procedure required precision and composure that were difficult to maintain, knowing how much was at stake.

With the necessary authorization in hand, the semen was extracted from its cryogenic environment. Every step of the thawing process was supervised with extreme care to avoid any possibility of contamination or DNA degradation that could compromise the analysis results.

Finally, the sample was prepared and analyzed vis-à-vis with the DNA found on Amarilis. This critical moment not only represented a potential turning point in the investigation but also carried intense emotional weight for Montesino, who faced the possibility of solving a case that had consumed so much of his energy and emotional resources. The wait for the results was a period of acute anxiety and anticipation, where every second seemed to stretch indefinitely.

After an agonizing wait of two weeks, during which Alfredo Montesino could barely contain his anxiety, the results of the genetic analysis finally arrived from a prestigious reference laboratory in the United States. Each day of waiting had been a whirlwind of emotions and planning, including preparations for a much-needed vacation on the idyllic island of Moorea, a Polynesian paradise that Alfredo had promised to revisit once the case was solved.

The document containing the results of the analysis was opened with trembling hands but filled with hope. The test, conducted with the utmost scientific precision, conclusively proved beyond any reasonable doubt that the semen samples recovered from Amarilis's body and those stored by Dr. Leo matched by 99.9%. The implications of this finding were clear and conclusive: Dr. Leo Salazar was unequivocally responsible for Amarilis's murder.

This confirmation fell like a hammer on Montesino's desk, solidifying all his suspicions and investigative efforts into an undeniable truth. The doctor, with all his education and facade of respectability, was a murderer. Justice, which seemed so elusive during the investigation, finally manifested in the most irrefutable way possible: DNA evidence.

The conclusion of this analysis not only marked the end of a turbulent chapter in the quest for justice for Amarilis but also allowed Montesino to close the case with the certainty that the perpetrator would not go unpunished. With a heavy heart for the victim's memory and relieved by the resolution of the case, Alfredo began to prepare for his trip to Moorea, a journey that now symbolized the closure and the beginning of a necessary period of recovery and reflection after such a challenging and emotional case.

Twenty-four hours after the laboratories in the United States sent that unequivocal genetic result, which pointed to Dr. Leo Salazar as Amarilis's murderer, the machinery of justice began to move with relentless determination. An arrest warrant was issued without delay, and the doctor, faced with overwhelming evidence of his own guilt, soon admitted to the horrendous acts he had committed.

In an act of resignation and perhaps understanding the futility of denying the undeniable in the face of DNA scientific precision, Dr. Leo chose to accept a severe sentence. He voluntarily accepted a ninety-nine-year sentence for the crimes of murder, kidnapping, and mutilation, thus closing the legal chapter of his life with an ending marked by confinement and remorse.

Meanwhile, in a place where olives may cease to grow and stones may no longer have memory of the sun that warmed them, Amarilis's parents faced the painful process of closing the emotional wounds inflicted by their daughter's brutal murder. With the certainty that justice had been served, they could finally organize a burial ceremony worthy of Amarilis's memory. In a small humble church in their village, surrounded by several neighbors and few loved ones, they carried out a ceremony laden with sadness but also with some relief, knowing that earthly justice had been served.

Thus, Amarilis was laid to rest in a quiet corner of the local cemetery, under the shade of cypress trees that seemed to guard the secrets of those who rested there. Her parents placed a simple wooden cross on her grave, inscribing on it an epitaph that spoke of love and loss, of life and of justice restored. In that sacred place, they offered prayers for her soul, hoping that in some other world, in some other reality, Amarilis could find the peace that was so cruelly taken from her here.

Alfredo Montesino booked his plane ticket using the airline 'Tahiti Nui' with its beautiful Tiare flower stamp, destined for Tahiti, the birthplace of skin tattoos, followed by a ferry to the sublime island of Moorea.

***

About the Author

Born on April 14, 1954, in San Juan, Puerto Rico, Dr. Humberto Lugo Vicente, better known as Tito Lugo, is a distinguished figure in the field of pediatric surgery. His career has been distinguished by a fervent commitment to both medicine and the community he serves.

During his education at Colegio San José de Río Piedras, Dr. Lugo Vicente not only excelled in his studies but also led the local rock band "The Red Stones." He demonstrated exceptional skills in areas as varied as music and martial arts, where he achieved black belts in Shotokan and brown belts in Taekwondo. His determination to finance his karate education through newspaper sales and other jobs reflects his early commitment to his goals.

A graduate of the University of Puerto Rico Magna Cum Laude in Science, specializing in Chemistry and Biochemistry, Dr. Lugo Vicente was recognized with the Chemistry Medal and the Facundo Bueso Medal for his outstanding academic performance. He continued to shine in his medical studies at the same university, graduating as a member of Alpha Omega Alpha, the medical honor society.

Dr. Lugo Vicente has made a milestone in pediatric surgery throughout his career. He completed his specialization in General and Pediatric Surgery at the University of Puerto Rico. He then joined the faculty as Professor of Pediatric Surgery. His commitment to excellence in education led him to hold several leadership positions, including President of the Medical Faculty and Director of the Department of Surgery at the University Pediatric Hospital.

Dr. Lugo Vicente has been a tireless advocate for improving medical services in Puerto Rico, especially in his fight to equip the University Pediatric Hospital with modern operating rooms. This has benefited countless children and families.

Outside of his medical career, he enjoys an enriching family life with his wife Wanda Torres Otero and their four children: Karlos, Alex, Javier, and María del Carmen. His dedication to community well-being and his passion for medicine continue to be a source of inspiration for new generations.

Currently, Dr. Lugo Vicente practices in his private practice at Hospital San Jorge and the University Pediatric Hospital. There, he provides quality medical care while cultivating his interests in sports, writing, and oenology, always maintaining the balance and moderation that characterize his philosophy of life.

Other Novels by the Author

https://www.amazon.com/author/titolugo.md
https://www.lulu.com/spotlight/titolugomd

1- Aquamistic (Spanish and English)
2- El Gran Sueño / The Great Dream
3- Marca de Faraón / Mark of Pharaoh
4- La Isla del Retiro / The Island of Retirement
5- Espejismos en la Red / Digital Deceptions
6- Voces del Silencio / Voices of Silence
7- Travos… (Spanish and English)
8- Misericordia Letal / Lethal Mercy
9- Pirulo… (Spanish and English)
10- …Elipsis… / …Ellipsis…
11- Precognición / Precognition
12- Simpronio… (Spanish and English)
13- Travesía del Destino
14- El Escritor Olvidado
15- Journey Through Fate
16- The Forgotten Writer

* * *

www.ingramcontent.com/pod-product-compliance
Lightning Source LLC
Chambersburg PA
CBHW071159240526
45470CB00017B/385